Today's evangelicals actually se
They *like* it when the trumpet
critiques are taboo. Colin Eakin ....
contravening that taboo—sounding warnings with clarity and
emphasis, yet without sounding mean-spirited or disrespectful. His
analyses of popular theological errors never fail to instruct and
edify.

Phil Johnson
Executive Director, *Grace to You*

Dr. Eakin addresses one of the most difficult tasks of church
leaders—confronting false teaching. He provides guidance that is
drawn on the Scriptures and wise voices from the past.

Jason K. Lee, Ph.D.
Dean and Professor of Theological Studies
Cedarville University

Warning believers of false doctrine and false teachers is an oft-
repeated mandate in Scripture and yet very few take this mandate
seriously and fewer still do it properly. In his absolutely superb
book, *Beware of Dogs*, Colin Eakin shows us how to do both. As one
whose ministry is actively engaged in this task, I simply cannot
recommend this book to you highly enough.

Justin Peters
Justin Peters Ministries

Beware of the Dogs presents a clear and cogent summary of
prevalent errors in the church today. It will undoubtedly be a great
resource for pastors and laypeople alike in an age which suffers
from much confusion concerning the gospel. Colin Eakin's robust
yet gracious confrontation of error is highly recommended.

Paul Twiss
Instructor of Biblical Exposition
The Master's Seminary

The
EQUIP
Series

Beware of Dogs
Exposing Error in the Modern Church

Colin Eakin

WITH ALL WISDOM PUBLICATIONS
Cupertino, California

Dedicated to my pastor and friend,
Dr. Cliff McManis

Sagacious apologist,
Intrepid polemicist,
Worthy Sword-bearer

Contents

Acknowledgements

A number of people were instrumental in bringing about this publication, to whom I am profoundly indebted. This includes the entire team at WITH ALL WISDOM PUBLICATIONS, especially Series Editor Derek Brown, Associate Editors J. R. Cuevas, Breanna Paniagua, Jasmine Patton, and Proofreader Sergio Gonzalez. Special thanks to Oluwasanya Awe for his help with the cover design.

Thanks to Pastor John Fast of Hilltop Bible Church, Arrington, TN for his editorial insights.

I am very grateful to Phil Johnson, not only for contributing the Foreword, but also for hosting me at his blog, *Pyromaniacs*, thus providing a wider audience for these polemical ripostes over the past year two years.

Many additional thanks to Cliff McManis, whose imprint here involves not only his textual additions and clarifications, but also his faithful shepherding of my family and me, including some of the finest biblical instruction to be found anywhere. The book's dedication to him is a small commemoration for his role in my life.

Finally, a deep measure of appreciation to my wife, Michelle, whose wisdom and encouragement is ever present and invaluable to me in all my pursuits.

FOREWORD

Conflict is rightfully distasteful to all sane and sober-minded people. Anyone who takes delight in disputing with others is to be avoided. The apostle Paul regularly condemns quarrelsome people—those who have "**an unhealthy craving for controversy and for quarrels about words**" (**1 Tim 6:4**). He says they are puffed up with conceit and lacking in understanding—and he links that attitude with false teaching and an ungodly character (**v. 3**). **Proverbs 17:19** says lovers of strife are also lovers of transgression.

On the other hand, those who genuinely love the truth have a clear biblical mandate (and a solemn duty) to *contend earnestly* "**for the faith that was once for all delivered to the saints**" (**Jude 3**). The apostle Paul says a life "**worthy of the gospel of Christ**" entails "**standing firm . . . striving side by side for the faith of the gospel**" (**Phil 1:27**). True and faithful gospel ministry must sometimes be done "**in the midst of much conflict**" (**1 Thess 2:2**). In fact, conflict is inevitable if we are serious about following Christ. Jesus said, "**If the world hates you, know that it has hated me before it hated you. If you were of the world, the world would love you as its own; but because you are not of the world, but I chose you out of the world, therefore the world hates you**" (**John 15:18-19**). And "**in the world you will have tribulation**" (**v. 33**).

Scripture is chock full of reminders that all faithful Christians will face fierce opposition from the world. "**Indeed, all who desire to live a godly life in Christ Jesus**

will be persecuted" (**2 Tim 3**). And we are not to try to avoid that persecution or court the secular world's favor and friendship by adopting its values, beliefs, or opinions. That would be a form of spiritual adultery (**James 4:4**)—and treason.

All true followers of Christ in this fallen realm should understand that we are in a state of perpetual warfare. The warfare motif is a thread that runs through both Old and New Testaments. The history of Old Testament Israel is a long chronicle of both conquests and defeats—revealing a pattern of unrelenting conflicts between sin and righteousness; evil against good; and the schemes of men versus the will of God.   In the New Testament, Paul's counsel to Timothy included numerous admonitions telling him that he must view himself as a soldier: "**Wage the good warfare**" (**1 Tim 1:18**). "**Fight the good fight of the faith**" (**v. 12**). "**Share in suffering as a good soldier of Christ Jesus**" (**2 Tim 2:3**). "**Put on the whole armor of God**" (**Eph 6:11**).

It was never an appropriate stratagem for the people of God to try to appease their oppressors. "**Those who forsake the law praise the wicked, but those who keep the law strive against them**" (**Prov 28:4**). Jesus Himself said, "**Do not think that I have come to bring peace to the earth. I have not come to bring peace, but a sword**" (**Matt 10:34**). He went still further: "**Do you think that I have come to give peace on earth? No, I tell you, but rather division. For from now on in one house there will be five divided, three against two and two against three. They will be divided, father against son and son against father, mother against daughter and daughter against mother,**

mother-in-law against her daughter-in-law and daughter-in-law against mother-in-law" (Luke 12:51-53).

Life for faithful Christians will therefore inevitably include some measure of tribulation, distress, persecution, or danger—and sometimes even the enemy's sword (**Rom 8:35**). The believer, however, is not to be the one wielding a sword. "**The weapons of our warfare are not of the flesh**" (**2 Cor 10:4**). Our warfare is a *spiritual* and *ideological* battle, not a war against visible foes: "**We do not wrestle against flesh and blood, but against the rulers, against the authorities, against the cosmic powers over this present darkness, against the spiritual forces of evil in the heavenly places**" (**Eph 6:12**). In fact, the chief enemies we seek to destroy are not people, but *ideas*—false doctrines, carnal philosophies, evil ideologies, unbiblical worldviews, and anti-Christian opinions: "**We destroy arguments and every lofty opinion raised against the knowledge of God, and take every thought captive to obey Christ**" (**2 Cor 10:5**). People who are entangled in or enslaved by those errors are not the enemy; they are our mission field. Therefore, Paul says, "**The Lord's servant must not be quarrelsome but kind to everyone, able to teach, patiently enduring evil, *correcting his opponents with gentleness***" (**2 Tim 2:24-25**; emphasis added). Peter agrees: "**Honor Christ the Lord as holy, always being prepared to make a defense to anyone who asks you for a reason for the hope that is in you; *yet do it with gentleness and respect***" (**1 Pet 3:15**; emphasis added). Scripture tells us repeatedly that gentleness is to be the hallmark of our polemical conflicts.

Let's be candid: It is not easy for most of us to be both earnest and gentle while contending for the faith. It is not easy to hold in tension our duties as soldiers along with our

Lord's admonition to love our enemies. But in **2 Corinthians 10:3-5** Paul explains the whole point: our aim is not to destroy erring and unregenerate people, but to free them from the strongholds of delusion and sin in which they have become imprisoned.

I love theology, and I especially enjoy studying the history and development of Christian doctrine. Historical theology is one long chronicle of doctrinal polemics, spanning the entire Church Age. There has always been fierce controversy within the church over doctrine—including some long and rigorous polemical wars between professing Christians. And the church's understanding of truth and sound doctrine has always been advanced through polemics. The record of these controversies more than vindicates the absolute necessity of Jude's exhortation to contend earnestly for the faith.

But even the best of saints have sometimes failed to do this with gentleness and respect. Martin Luther's comments about the purveyors of false doctrine were sometimes too vulgar to bear repeating. His preference for scatological insults is well documented. Even his milder remonstrations were often deliberately insulting. For example (and this is a fairly mild one), in a book written against the opinions held by followers of his own former colleague, Luther wrote, "Their interpretation is so stupid that it makes one feel like vomiting."[1] He routinely used the term *teufelsdreck* ("devil's filth") as a pejorative to describe any teaching that contradicted Lutheran doctrine. He wrote, "Whatever is not in agreement with [sound doctrine] must be called the devil's

---

[1] Helmut T. Lehmann and Conrad Bergenddoff, eds., *Luther's Works [vol. 40]: Church and Ministry II,* "Against the Heavenly Prophets in the Matter of Images and Sacraments, 1525" (Minneapolis: Fortress, 1958), 187.

filth and must be swept out of the church."[2] And when he disagreed with other Reformers (including John Calvin, Heinrich Bullinger, and especially Ulrich Zwingli) he argued with similar vehemence.

Other Protestant luminaries (including Calvin) have likewise sometimes used intemperate language in their polemical writings. It is an easy trap to fall into (as anyone who has sought to refute damnable heresies will attest). But Calvin usually demonstrated a more Christ-like spirit, and he clearly understood the dangers of overheated polemical zeal. In a letter to Bullinger, he wrote:

> I hear that Luther has at length broken forth in fierce invective, not so much against you as against the whole of us. On the present occasion, I dare scarce venture to ask you to keep silence, because it is neither just that innocent persons should thus be harassed, nor that they should be denied the opportunity of clearing themselves; neither, on the other hand, is it easy to determine whether it would be prudent for them to do so. But of this I do earnestly desire to put you in mind, in the first place, that you would consider how eminent a man Luther is, and the excellent endowments wherewith he is gifted, with what strength of mind and resolute constancy, with how great skill, with what efficiency and power of doctrinal statement, he hath hitherto devoted his whole energy to overthrow the reign of Antichrist, and at the same

---

[2] Helmut. T. Lehmann, ed., *Luther's Works [vol. 22]: Sermons on St. John* (St. Louis: Concordia, 1968), 434.

time to diffuse far and near the doctrine of salvation. Often have I been wont to declare, that even although he were to call me a devil, I should still not the less hold him in such honor that I must acknowledge him to be an illustrious servant of God. But while he is endued with rare and excellent virtues, he labors at the same time under serious faults. Would that he had rather studied to curb this restless, uneasy temperament which is so apt to boil over in every direction. I wish, moreover, that he had always bestowed the fruits of that vehemence of natural temperament upon the enemies of the truth, and that he had not flashed his lightning sometimes also upon the servants of the Lord. Would that he had been more observant and careful in the acknowledgment of his own vices. Flatterers have done him much mischief, since he is naturally too prone to be over-indulgent to himself. . . . Besides, you will do yourselves no good by quarreling, except that you may afford some sport to the wicked, so that they may triumph not so much over us as over the Evangel. If they see us rending each other asunder, they then give full credit to what we say, but when with one consent and with one voice we preach Christ, they avail themselves unwarrantably of our inherent weakness to cast reproach upon our faith.[3]

---

3. Lehmann, *Luther's Works, [vol. 22]*: 432-34.

The Internet is currently well-salted with polemicists who seem enthralled with the spirit of Luther but heedless to the wiser counsel of Calvin—who is of course merely echoing the instruction of the apostle Paul: "**If you bite and devour one another, watch out that you are not consumed by one another**" (**Gal 5:15**).

For nearly a decade beginning in 2005, I helped author a blog where our main focus was to critique and challenge claims that were being made by a loosely organized movement that many referred to as "The Emerging Church." Of course I was aware of the New Testament's many admonitions against quarrelsomeness and overly harsh treatment of those in error, and my blog partners and I *did* try not to violate that principle. But (speaking for myself only) I am sure there were times when I ought to have been more charitable to my adversaries. I know some of our readers would say amen to that.

Unfortunately, most evangelicals today seem to think any earnest polemical engagement with error is inherently uncharitable. One of the few dogmas that postmoderns will permit is the idea that settled certainty (especially with regard to spiritual matters) is inherently arrogant—and therefore to say someone else's religious beliefs are wrong is considered the ultimate breach of charity and the very height of incivility, no matter how it is stated. The only thing still considered heresy is a firm commitment to the old orthodoxy. So it has become very difficult—well-nigh impossible—to deal with theological debates in a hearty polemical fashion without being accused of impertinence (or worse). Nowadays, even in the evangelical academy (perhaps I should say *especially* there), the common belief is that every point of theological disagreement must be counterbalanced by three or four statements of commendation. This has the effect of making every issue seem foggy. But today's evangelicals actually seem to prefer ambiguity to clarity. They *like* it when the trumpet gives an uncertain sound. So pure critiques are taboo.

Colin Eakin has mastered the art of contravening that taboo—sounding warnings with clarity and emphasis, yet without sounding mean-spirited or disrespectful. His analyses of popular theological errors never fail to instruct and edify. They reprove and rebuke, of course—sometimes sharply (**Titus 1:13**)—but with enough careful, cautious, biblical restraint that even the individual being critiqued should not feel insulted.

I had left blogging and my blog-partners all but fell silent after the Emerging Church movement more or less dissolved in 2012. But starting around 2014, many evangelicals began to adopt and promote a neo-Marxist idea of "social justice." By 2018 it had become the latest evangelical fad. It seemed to me that the rhetoric and many of the values of the social justice movement echoed the Emerging Church movement. So I reopened the blog and solicited entries from new contributors. Dr. Eakin was one of the first and finest volunteers who responded. The quality of his writing and the clarity of his arguments astonished me. He is neither an ordained pastor nor a career theologian, but his grasp of theology and his ability to communicate and teach are superlative.

This collection of his essays is well worth reading. I am pleased to see these articles brought together in this format, printed in hard-copy, and preserved in book form. I know you will be challenged, edified, encouraged, and greatly helped by his insights.

I am profoundly thankful for his contributions to the blog, and I am excited for the impact I believe this book can have. **"A gentle tongue can** [still] **break a bone" (Prov 25:15)**.

Phil Johnson
Executive Director, *Grace to You*
December 2019

Introduction
Beware of Dogs!

"Look out for the dogs, look out for the evildoers, look out for those who mutilate the flesh" (Phil 3:2)

It is my guess this verse was not the basis for many church sermons last Sunday. In fact, it is likely the rare (and long-time) churchgoer who has ever had any explicit instruction on it. This is understandable from a human perspective. After all, the gist of the verse is undeniably pejorative. It resorts to name-calling, and of an especially derogatory sort. It warns of evildoers, implying the writer (the Apostle Paul) does not share that distinction and so potentially subjects himself to charges of judgmentalism and hypocrisy. Not only that, its relevance might be called into question, for who today is seeking to **"mutilate the flesh?"**

So why is this verse in the Bible? More to the point, who would highlight it as a sermon subject, or even more outlandishly, use it as the basis for a book? To call one's opponents **"dogs"** might seem to many readers unnecessarily provocative, even incendiary. Isn't Paul forgetting here his admonition from **Colossians 4:6**, that all speech is to be **"gracious"** and **"seasoned with salt?"** Isn't he violating what he wrote to Timothy, **"...the Lord's servant must not be quarrelsome but kind to everyone?"** (**2 Tim 2:24**). How is this language in **Philippians 3:2** gracious and kind? Surely—you might be wondering—there must be a more tactful and applicable theme verse for a book on equipping the modern Christian. And would a gentle and loving God approve of such language?

Answer: absolutely and unequivocally. The language is *God's*. This verse is God's inerrant, enduring and unapologetic wording, as much as any other verse in the Bible (**Prov 30:5**). Here, as in all places in Scripture, God perfectly inspires Paul's thoughts to write exactly *what* He deems should be said, and *how* it should be said (**2 Tim 3:16**). It is the Holy Spirit who says to "**beware of dogs.**" It is the Holy Spirit who describes them as "**evildoers.**" And it is the Holy Spirit who depicts these evildoing dogs to be avoided as those who "**mutilate the flesh.**" What has the Holy Spirit so incensed? Why the stridency? It is because this baleful canine menace was striking at the core of God's fundamental message to the world. How so? To understand this, we must delve a little deeper into what concerned Paul as he wrote to the Philippians.

Paul's letter to the Philippians was likely written sometime during his first imprisonment in Rome, around A.D. 60 or 61. The church in Philippi had been established nearly a decade earlier during Paul's second missionary journey. Dogging him as he traveled on that journey and seeking to subvert his teaching within the churches he founded were members of a troublemaking sect known as Judaizers. Why were they such trouble to Paul? At first blush, the reason might not be readily apparent. After all, the Judaizers believed Jesus Christ is the Son of God. Not only that, they believed Christ's death and resurrection paved the way for forgiveness of sins. So what was the problem?

The problem with the Judaizers lay in their insistence that true believers must not only believe in the Person and work of Jesus Christ, *but also* comply with Jewish religious customs in order to be saved (**Acts 15:1, 5**). For them, Judaism was the vestibule by which to enter Christianity.[4] The term "**mutilate the flesh**" references the Jewish ceremonial custom of circumcision, which was being misrepresented by the Judaizers as a vital condition for salvation, rather than as a symbolic representation of God's cleansing of the inner part (i.e. the soul) from sin (**Deut 10:6; 30:6; Jer 4:4**). This teaching lay in stark contrast to the true message of the gospel, bringing salvation through repentance and faith in Christ's substitutionary death and resurrection *alone*. The heresy of adding works to faith in salvation so riled Paul that he wrote an entire letter to the churches in Galatia alerting them to this error. His denunciation of those adding anything to God's singular and wondrous manner of redemption reaches a crescendo in the fifth chapter, where he warns, "**Look: I, Paul, say to you that if you accept circumcision, Christ will be of no value to you...you are severed from Christ...you have fallen away from grace**" (**Gal 5:2, 4**). According to Paul, add anything to faith as the means of salvation and the saving effect of faith is nullified. It is in this same context that the Holy Spirit directs Paul's use of the harsh epithets in **Philippians 3:2** against similarly minded culprits in Philippi seeking to falsify God's criteria for salvation.

Circumcision has since faded from the scene as a primary battleground between the true and the false over salvation, but don't be fooled into thinking the threat it represented is

---

[4] John MacArthur, from the sermon, "The Importance of Doctrinal Courage," Grace Community Church, Sun Valley, CA, March 9, 2019. https://www.gty.org/library/sermons-library/SC18-3/the-importance-of-doctrinal-courage

dormant. The spirit of the Judaizers lives on today in a myriad of contemporary heresies having the same effect as the Judaizers of Paul's day—undermining the gospel via adding works to faith in salvation. The words of one prominent pastor in the mainstream of today's evangelical Christianity are representative of many when he says, "Every step you make takes you one step closer to heaven, or one step closer to hell." His implication? What humans do in their moment-by-moment daily decisions impacts their acceptability by God. This is rank heresy as much today as in Paul's time, and undoubtedly would have incited the same heated rhetoric Paul used with the Galatians. Yet sadly (and absurdly), many current churchgoers who fashion themselves as subservient to biblical authority sit cluelessly week in and week out as they ingest this and other heretical instruction.

And so we arrive at the purpose of this book: to awaken a generally torpid and negligent modern evangelical church out of its doctrinal stupor. In particular, it is designed to reassert the clear gospel—**"the power of God for salvation to everyone who believes" (Rom 1:16)**—and contrast it against several of its present day corruptions. As one insightful pastor comments upon **Philippians 3:2**, "Any attempt to please God by one's own efforts and draw attention away from Christ's accomplished redemption is the worst kind of wickedness."[5] This book seeks to counter such wickedness. As in Paul's era, modern day believers must be warned against **"dogs"** and **"evildoers"** who still seek to distort the gospel by adding human achievement to God's work in salvation.

[5] John MacArthur, note on Phil 3:2, *The MacArthur Study Bible*, English Standard (Wheaton: Crossway, 2010), 1825.

This book is therefore by nature *polemical*. Polemics is that field of theology dealing with the denunciation of falsehood. It is related to but different from the complementary field of *apologetics*, which deals with the defense of truth. One can think of the inter-relation between the two in the dual uses of a sword in combat: (1) to parry and to deflect blows in defense (apologetics), and (2) to thrust and to strike on offense (polemics). Apologetics seeks to defend what is true while polemics seeks to attack what is false; both are vital Christian tactics commissioned by God in His Word (**1 Pet 3:15; 2 Tim 4:2; Titus 1:9, 13; 2:15**). The supreme Exemplar of polemics in Scripture is none other than the Lord Jesus Christ, who modeled its proper use in His sundry attacks against the counterfeit teaching of the lawyers, scribes and religious leaders of His day (**Matt 23:13-36; Luke 11:42, 52**; discussed in greater detail in the Conclusion). John the Baptist, whom Jesus held up as a paragon of virtue (**Matt 11:11**), was also proficient in the area of polemics, targeting both the religious (**Matt 3:7-12**) and the secular (**Mark 6:14-29**). Other New Testament figures demonstrating polemical proficiency under the inspiration of the Holy Spirit include Peter (**Acts 2:36-40; 2 Pet 2:1-3:10**), Paul (**Gal 1:6-8**), the Apostle John (**2 John 7-11; 3 John 9**), the writer of Hebrews (**Heb 10:26-31**), James (**James 4:1-10**), Jude (**Jude 1-23**) and Stephen (**Acts 7:51-60**).

The main goal of polemics is to identify and denounce the falsehoods of the enemy, Satan, whom Jesus calls the "**father of lies**" (**John 8:44**). Because Satan perpetually seeks to undermine God's truth and so endanger His flock, polemics will remain a vital spiritual armament in the lives of believers until his ultimate demise. In a sense, the biblical art of polemics works similarly to how an Internal Affairs division operates within a police force, or how the Securities and Exchange Commission (SEC) oversees the stock markets. Because police departments and Wall Street trading houses are staffed by humans subject to the same omnipresent temptations to wrongdoing as anywhere else, agents within Internal Affairs and the SEC maintain vigilant oversight and prosecute offenses to ensure the well-being of the wider community they are sanctioned to protect. Such is the work of polemics within God's Church—it seeks to ensure the spiritual well-being of Christ's flock by countering error as it arises.

The analogy goes a step further. Just as agents in Internal Affairs or the SEC are often regarded as pariahs by those under surveillance, polemicists in the Church today are far more likely to incite resistance and recrimination than acceptance and appreciation for their work. Rather than being thanked for their spiritual discernment and oversight, polemicists are commonly subject to charges of divisiveness, judgmentalism, egotism, highhandedness, hypocrisy, bitterness, hyper-criticism and assorted other misanthropic and schismatic motives.

So if this is true, then why write a polemical book? Why subject oneself to such attacks? There are four biblical reasons for doing so:

(1) *Well-being of believers.* Polemics is designed chiefly to protect Christ's flock. Paul prefaces **Philippians 3:2** by saying, **"To write the same things to you is no trouble for me *and is safe for you***" (**Phil 3:1b**; italics added). Paul's emphasis is the spiritual safety of his readers, and his point is this: believers need to be continually apprised of spiritual threats seeking to undermine the truth of how God saves sinners. Jesus warned of figurative **"robbers,"** **"thieves,"** and

"**wolves**" who would seek to plunder His flock via deception after His departure (**John 10:1-13**). Over time, God has used His polemicists to counter this threat. In addition to those listed above, Augustine, Athanasius, Luther, Calvin, Knox, Owen, Edwards, Whitfield, Warfield, Spurgeon, Lloyd-Jones, Sproul and MacArthur are just some among many God has used through the centuries to fight deception and preserve orthodox biblical understanding among His followers.[6]

(2) *Well-being of polemicist(s)*. Gospel proclamation is the responsibility of all who are born again. But certain believers are especially gifted by God for the furtherance of His truth. To these are given the spiritual gifts of preaching, teaching, knowledge, wisdom and discernment. When God grants such gifts to His followers, He expects these leaders to be faithful to their charge. Reward is given to those who are valiant in the task, and punishment to those who falter (**Matt 25:14-30; Luke 19:11-27**). In the Old Testament, God even assigns the punishment of the wicked upon the "watchman" who fails to caution the wayward as he should. At the same time, God assures the polemicist, "**if you warn the wicked, and he does not turn from his wickedness, or from his wicked way, he shall die for his iniquity, but you will have delivered your soul**" (**Ezek 3:18-19**). Clearly, God places a tremendous burden of disclosure upon those to whom He grants insight into His Word. Note also that it is faithfulness in the discharge of polemical duty which concerns God, and not whether the warning is heeded. The prophet Jeremiah is a

---

[6] For a discussion of how the gospel essentials were codified, defended and preserved well before Martin Luther ignited the Reformation, see Busenitz, Nathan, *Long Before Luther: Tracing the Heart of the Gospel from Christ to the Reformation* (Chicago, IL: Moody Publishers, 2017), and Lawson, Steven, *Foundations of Grace*, vol. 1 and 2 (Sanford, FL: Reformation Trust, 2008).

classic example of a godly polemicist who faithfully warned of coming judgment despite zero evident desired response from his audience.

(3) *Well-being of perpetrators.* While perhaps not as obvious, there is a third biblical rationale for polemics, and that is the well-being of its target(s). As with any Christian effort, all godly polemics must be done with a heart of love and an intent to bless, and this extends even toward the false teacher. Here it is important to recall Paul's admonition that any task not done in love is spiritually fruitless (**1 Cor 13:1-3**). Therefore, the godly polemicist must always have a loving regard for the one being taken to task for spiritual error. How is this possible? Because polemicists war not against any particular *person*, but rather against the *error* that person is promulgating. It is in this sense that Jude says to "**have mercy on those who doubt; save others by snatching them out of the fire; to others show mercy with fear, hating even the garment stained by the flesh**" (**Jude 22-23**). In other words, salvation must be the desire of the biblical polemicist, even for the one teaching error.

For this to happen, humility must suffuse all polemical undertakings. The godly polemicist remains perpetually cognizant of Paul's admonition in **1 Corinthians 4:7**: "**What do you have that you did not receive?**" No one can interpret Scripture—and in particular discern truth from error—apart from the Spirit's illumination (**1 Cor 2:6-16**). Mindfulness of this reality will keep the godly polemicist from descending to prideful postures and boorish behaviors. It is only by correcting opponents with humility, gentleness and kindness that, "**God may perhaps grant them** [i.e. those caught in error] **repentance leading to a knowledge of the truth, and they may come to their senses and escape** from the snare of the devil, after being captured by him to do his will" (2 Tim 2:25-26).

(4) *Obedience to God.* The fourth rationale for pursuing polemics is the most fundamental: out of obedience to God. It is God who warns against being, "...children, tossed to and fro by the waves and carried about by every wind of doctrine, by human cunning, by craftiness in deceitful schemes" (Eph 4:14). To guard against this, God says to, "...charge certain persons not to teach any different doctrine" (1 Tim 1:3). And when they do? The Spirit's instruction is blunt: "Take no part in the unfruitful works of darkness, but instead expose them" (Eph 5:11). God even unveils the nature and weapons of the polemical quest when He speaks through the hand of Paul, "For though we walk in the flesh, we are not waging war according to the flesh. For the weapons of our warfare are not of the flesh but have divine power to destroy strongholds" (2 Cor 10:3-4). The following verse then hones in on the essence of polemics: "We destroy arguments and every lofty opinion raised against the knowledge of God, and take every thought captive to obey Christ" (2 Cor 10:5). That is, in a nutshell, the polemical directive: to decimate those ideas, arguments and opinions opposed to the knowledge of God, as found in His Word, so that all thoughts within the Lord's Church might be Christ's own. With such a clear and compelling command, believers have no option but to obey.

So how did this divine polemical charge become manifest in the book you now hold in your hands? In 2018, the Pew Research Center reported that 52 % of American Protestants believe good works in addition to faith are necessary for salvation.[7] According to God in His Word, this belief is damning (**Deut 27:26; Gal 3:10-11; 5:2-4**). Citing this statistic in his concluding address at the 2018 Shepherds' Conference, Pastor John MacArthur asked who in this generation would arise to denounce such error and defend the true gospel. Around the same time, Phil Johnson, Executive Director of *Grace to You*, exhumed his popular polemical blog site *Pyromaniacs,* at least in part to combat the ascendency of "social justice" and other aberrancies within the modern evangelical church (we discuss this topic at length in Chapters 4 and 5). In so doing, he welcomed likeminded contributors who shared his concern for the doctrinal drift within modern evangelicalism. What followed were a series of articles I penned in late 2018 and early 2019 designed to highlight a number of these contemporary incursions against historic Christian orthodoxy, and especially those undermining the gospel. Detecting a theme, my friend and pastor Dr. Cliff McManis encouraged me to unite these articles into a book on discernment (or lack thereof) in the modern Church.

As we have done previously, throughout this book all biblical quotes and references are in bold. This is done chiefly to prioritize Scripture above commentary and to facilitate ready recognition of God's own words. In **Psalm 138:2b,** God declares, "**You have exalted above all things Your name and Your Word**." Highlighting Scriptural passages in this manner symbolically elevates the words of God to their proper place and emphasizes the uniqueness and importance of divine revelation.

In warning His people in the Old Testament, God denounces false teaching "**dogs**," calling them "**blind**" and

---

[7] https://www.pewforum.org/2017/08/31/u-s-protestants-are-not-defined-by-reformation-era-controversies-500-years-later/

claiming they are **"shepherds who have no understanding"** and are **"all without knowledge"** (Isa 56:10-11). This passage from Isaiah was likely on Paul's mind as he warned of the same situation in **Philippians 3:2**, and similar false **"dogs"** persist even to this day. It is my hope in the following pages you will be apprised of contemporary efforts from within the Church to undermine the one true gospel and other truths from God's Word, in order that you might be motivated and equipped to oppose these assaults.

1

Beware False Scheming

Screwtape Revisited: How to Build
a Whitewashed Tomb

"Woe to you, scribes and Pharisees, hypocrites! For you are like whitewashed tombs, which outwardly appear beautiful, but within are full of dead people's bones and all uncleanness" (Matt 23:27)

In 1942, Englishman C.S. Lewis published a book entitled *The Screwtape Letters*. In it, a senior devil named Screwtape details to his nephew and underling, Wormwood, methods for waylaying and ultimately damning his intended victim. The book is a clever and revealing look at how the actual devil, Satan, goes about perpetrating his odious work in the world. One overarching theme behind Screwtape's instruction to Wormwood is how the subtle provocation away from truth is usually more helpful in bringing souls to hell than blatant exposures to deplorable sins. Writes Screwtape to his young apprentice, "Indeed the safest road to Hell is the gradual one—the gentle slope, soft underfoot, without sudden turnings, without milestones, without signposts...."

One glance across the landscape of professing Christianity since the book's publication shows how Satan has capitalized mightily on Screwtape's insight, using incremental apostasy to poison the well of doctrinal truth and undermine the Church's message. Incremental nudges away from biblical fidelity are the hallmark of the false church, and the chief exponents Satan has employed for this task have been the contemporary equivalents of the "**scribes and Pharisees**" of Jesus' day, those tasked with overseeing scriptural instruction. Christ's no-holds-barred denunciation of such false teachers was designed to expose these counterfeit religious leaders for who they really are—walking sepulchers housing spiritual cadavers.

Why "**whitewashed?**" Because Jesus knew what His Spirit would later inspire the Apostle Paul to write (**2 Cor 11:13-15**): "**For such men are false apostles, deceitful workmen, disguising themselves as apostles of Christ. And no wonder, for even Satan disguises himself as an angel of light. So it is no surprise if his servants, also, disguise themselves as servants of righteousness.**" The "wolf in sheep's clothing" (**Matt 7:13-14; Acts 20:28**) has been Satan's chief ploy for deceiving the unsuspecting since the early days of the Church. Christ's diatribe in **Matthew 23:27** is meant to warn of the spiritual leader housed in a sincere, winsome, wholesome-appearing, religiously adorned exterior, all the while concealing a spiritual corpse. And what was true then holds true today: nothing infuriates God more than a theologian or spiritual teacher whose pestilent instruction is hidden by a veneer of respectability and charm, with just enough feints towards orthodoxy to beguile the naive. Moreover, knowing that students ultimately become like their masters (**Luke 6:40**), Christ wanted all to know what was at stake given continued exposure to such impostors and their fetid deceit.

But despite the myriad of scriptural warnings to be on guard against such teachers, the sad reality is that the Church has never been as awash in falsehood as it is today. It is as if Satan has hit upon the "whitewashed tomb" as the principal means for furthering his deception, and is now doubling down on their production. So if a new edition of *The Screwtape Letters* were to be published today, we might imagine it would contain an addendum entitled, "How to Build a Whitewashed Tomb." If artifice and apostasy is to continue infiltrating the Church, then Wormwood must be updated on the furtherance of this chief tactic of Satan. With this in mind, let us imagine how Screwtape might write to Wormwood today:

My Dear Wormwood,

It being some time since our last correspondence, with developments both favorable and troubling, I feel compelled to write and bring you up to date on the latest directives from our Ruler. You will recall in prior posts I emphasized to you the value of incremental apostasy in undermining our Enemy's work. And no factor over the last two millennia has been more integral to this stratagem than the ongoing reproduction of (to use our Enemy's censorious term) "whitewashed tombs." As you know, these clandestine operatives appear to be working for *Him*, when in reality they are working for *us*.

That such a strategy has succeeded through the years, and even works today, is quite remarkable. For when our Enemy walked the earth, He plainly exposed our agents then for what they are—"whitewashed tombs"—and warned in great detail how they were to be identified (**Matt 7:13-14; 23:1-36; John 10:7-13**). Not only that, His inspired scribes revealed us—the instigators and motivators behind these agents—in our true form, as "**servants of righteousness**" (**2 Cor 11:13-15**). Such disclosures might have spelled disaster, as the impact of our counterfeit work lies in its spiritual camouflage, and here the Holy One of Israel was drawing back the curtain for all to see. Fortunately, time, vanity and spiritual lethargy have combined to dull the discernment of mankind to His warnings, to a degree that never before have our agents been so ubiquitous, and are finding greener pastures with every passing decade.

But we cannot become complacent. Remember how five centuries ago, the tide swung against us most dramatically and regrettably, and many souls were lost to the Enemy forever. It is uncertain we will ever fully recover from this calamity, as even now vestiges of that so-called "Reformation" continue to befuddle and undermine our labors. Therefore, you must understand our Ruler's prioritization of false teaching as our foremost task at hand, which in turn is predicated upon the replication of our prized "whitewashed tombs," that the unsuspecting might be permanently waylaid from the Truth. So without further ado, I pass along to you our Ruler's formula for how to build a "whitewashed tomb." If you can deceive the would-be teacher of the Word with these three simple measures, you will ensure their continued reproduction for the foreseeable future:

1. The "whitewashed tomb" will downplay the biblical description of spiritual death.

The first task in creating a whitewashed tomb is to obscure the biblical description of all mankind as being spiritually dead. As you know, the Enemy's Word is not ambiguous in declaring this as the true spiritual condition of all people prior to conversion. Fortunately, the world finds this doctrine especially scandalous, so we must naturally exploit their sense of insult. You will find your "tombs" will readily stray from teaching truth when it is offensive to their listeners. They will be loath to inform them that all humans are born into this world as spiritually deceased **"children of wrath"** (**Eph 2:1-3**), that they live under the contemporaneous judgment of God (**John 3:18; 36**), and that—apart from salvation via repentance and faith—they are headed to eternal torment in hell (**Matt 25:41, 46**). Let your would-be instructor teach that humans are broken, oppressed, hurt, needful, insufficient, helpless, or any other distressed condition, but never spiritually deceased. If your tomb or his audience were to learn this truth of their condition (**Ps 51:5; Matt 8:21-22; Luke 15:24; Eph 2:1, 5**), they would then be far likelier to yearn for the new life the Enemy offers through repentance and faith. Biblical terms and phrases we have sought to quash—such as "born again"—might reemerge and wreak havoc with our plans.

Critical to this, of course, is that our Enemy's Word must remain unopened, or if opened, then ignored. Have your minions quote mystics and spiritual sages in lieu of the Truth. And when the Word must be quoted (as you will find at times is necessary to promote our ruse), the text must serve the doctrinal presuppositions of our teachers, and not vice-versa. Your tombs should offer competing understandings of straightforward but culturally abhorrent passages, and disdain polemical and apologetic use of the Word as illegitimate "proof-texting." Whenever possible, have your tombs offer solace to those who find it hard to spend time in the Word, as though such activity is incidental for the "Jesus-follower" (a nice substitute for "Christian"). Favor small groups simply gathering to share their lives and offer each other support over any formal "Bible study." Above all, our subjects must remain ignorant of the Enemy's clear tactic, which He openly declared in **John 5:25**: **"Truly, truly, I say to you, an hour is coming, and is now here, when the dead will hear the voice of the Son of God, and those who hear will live."** We must do all we can to thwart such a development, and the key is to mislead the masses away from our Enemy's Word and its unambiguous truth—that all humanity is spiritually dead until some hear His voice and become alive.

2. *The "whitewashed tomb" will invert the biblical order of spiritual regeneration.*

Unfortunately, my dear Nephew, it is inevitable that the sinner's need for rebirth by our Enemy will surface. Sooner or later, the guilt and shame of sin will weigh on some, and they will long for spiritual regeneration which only our Enemy can provide. When that happens, it is imperative for you to invert the order of spiritual transformation. What do I mean? Simply this: humans must be encouraged to believe what they do for God makes them acceptable before God. They must be taught that one's performance for God determines his or her position with God, that one can belong to Him before one believes in Him.

This is, of course, baldly refuted throughout Scripture. You know, dear Wormwood, that our Enemy calls the prayers and other acts of service done by those who have not yet been redeemed by Him through repentance and faith an "**abomination**" (**Prov 15:8; 28:9; Isa 64:6**). In fact, this is nothing other than legalism, that old tried and true tactic perfected by the Pharisees, yet still a compelling vice all these years later. This falsehood remains enticing because sinners warm to the idea that they might offer works to be approved by our Enemy, and recoil at being told they can do nothing to merit His acceptance. The endurance and even flourishing of legalism explains how much of the professing Church today is bursting with spiritual activity and service rendered to our Enemy with absolutely no clue how to be truly reconciled to Him (2 Cor 5:18-21).

You might think the biblical evidence opposing this legalistic heresy is too overwhelming for our ploy to work, but think again. Not long ago, a well-known megachurch pastor and popular author bemoaned to his congregation that, ". . . people are drawn to Buddhism rather than Christianity because they understand Buddhism to be a religion of practice, but Christianity to be a religion of beliefs. I don't know who defined Christianity that way, but it was not Jesus." As you know, dear Wormwood, it certainly was! The Gospel of John is a veritable treasure trove of quotes by our Enemy refuting this teacher's statement and demonstrating that salvation comes only from *believing*, with subsequent acts of righteousness only confirming the legitimacy of one's salvation (Eph 2:8-10; 2 Thess 2:13; James 2:14-18; this is, again, why we must do everything possible to distract people from the Word). As you know, the world of religions that we have spawned and even now sustain are all based upon the pretense that human effort can win the Almighty's approval. As long as sinners can be deceived away from the truth that right belief must precede right practice, we will ensure their spiritual confusion and, ultimately, their damnation.

3. The "whitewashed tomb" will ignore the biblical gospel of spiritual substitution.

Once your teacher ignores or, better yet, *denies* spiritual death as the default condition of all, then inverts the biblical order of spiritual regeneration by placing right practice ahead of right belief, your task is almost complete. The final nail in your whitewashed coffin is this: corruption of the true gospel through denial of penal substitutionary atonement.

As you know, the Enemy has clearly stated that salvation comes from believing the gospel (**Rom 1:16; 1 Cor 15:2-3**), and that the gospel basics—involving the death and resurrection of His Son—must be accepted according to the Scriptures (**1 Cor 15:2-4**). This means those who would be saved through repentance and belief in the gospel (**Mark 1:15**) must understand that gospel as the Bible has described it: a gospel borne out of sacrifice by One Man to save the many through His satisfaction of His Father's just wrath against sin (**Isa 53:4-12; Gal 3:13; 2 Cor 5:21; 1 John 2:2; 4:10**). By bearing the punishment for all those who would ever believe, the Son has forever redeemed them from the penalty their sin deserved (**1 Pet 2:24**).

Because faith in this reality is what permanently severs our link with the vulnerable soul, we must obscure with full exertion the truth spelled out above. Jesus' death must be presented in nebulous terms, as the ultimate example of self-sacrifice, or as some vague representation of victory over evil, or as evidence of mankind's infinite worth rather than his desperate need. Once sinners realize every sin must be punished by death, either through their own suffering for eternity or by Christ upon the cross, then the floodgates to salvation will be plain for all to see, and our cause will be doomed. Fortunately, our Ruler's rebranding of the gospel around "social justice" has been a most propitious development, as it reverses the sinner's orientation from abject petitioner for mercy from God into entitled protester for recompense from man. A large swath of professing believers is now so centered on earthly indemnification that they have complete ignorance of, and (even better) disinterest in, spiritual rebirth. May such a damning perspective checkmate indefinitely the Enemy's desire to bring sons and daughters to His glory (**Heb 2:10**).

There you have it, dear Nephew. Use this letter to redouble your efforts in perpetuating falsehood via the development of respectable crypts. Through rejection of the notion that the unredeemed are spiritually dead, reversal of the manner of spiritual regeneration, and repudiation of the need for spiritual substitution, you will become a master craftsman in your bid to transform today's spiritual teachers into "whitewashed tombs."

Your affectionate uncle,

Screwtape

2

Beware False Teachers
Sheep, or Wolf?

If you were asked to identify the Bible's most neglected command for the Christian today, how would you answer? Richard Stearns of World Vision has written that our greatest neglect—what he terms the "hole in our gospel"—is failure to address adequately the material needs of the world's less fortunate.[8] Is that true? Is this where Christians are most deserting Christ's work today?

Here is a survey of various mission projects and priorities featured on the websites of a random selection of Bay Area churches in recent years: homeless shelter, fair trade, sex trafficking, micro-lending to the Third World, food for the hungry, Africa relief, Haiti relief, flood relief, fire relief—the list goes on. Even a cursory glimpse of area churches across a wide spectrum of doctrinal beliefs shows a tremendous commitment to the downtrodden, to those most materially "at risk." There may be a "hole" in our outworking of true

---

[8]Richard Stearns, *The Hole in Our Gospel* (New York: Thomas Nelson, Inc., 2010), 3-8.

Christian faith, but it doesn't lie in inattention to the less fortunate. So if there is a so-called "hole," a most neglected biblical doctrine, where does it lie?

Looks Can Be *Very* Deceiving

As a hint, imagine this scenario. Maybe someone you know is alone, wandering in his own spiritual desert. Not only that, maybe he has unmet physical needs, maybe even actual hunger. To go even further, maybe to all appearances he cannot or will not recognize his innate capacity for success, his opportunity to exert his God-given aptitude for noteworthy accomplishment.

Then along comes someone of friendly countenance, one who is sensitive to the loner's difficulties. He appears on the scene just in time to encourage and uplift the forlorn stranger. He sees his hunger and provides an opportunity for food. He senses the loner's spiritual longing and encourages him with promises from Scripture. He grasps the unrecognized or unacknowledged potential in the loner and exhorts him to fulfill all that he is designed to be.

Pretty magnanimous, wouldn't you say? This would seem, at least on first glance, to mirror sound Christian practice in every sense. In fact, this outreach seems not unlike the Good Samaritan in action. He has come alongside the loner when no one else has or will. He has tended to the loner's physical, spiritual and psychological needs in a noble manner. And in so doing, he has walked in Jesus' footsteps, hasn't he? He has proven himself to be a true "Jesus-follower," right?

There's just one problem. The scenario outlined above is not hypothetical. This scenario actually happened and is recorded in the Bible. The loner described above is Jesus, as depicted in **Matthew 4:1-5**. The "friend" is Satan.

Whoa! What's going on here? How could this be? Isn't Satan always despicable in practice? Doesn't he only work in the realm of violence, hatred, wickedness, perversity and other forms of obvious evil? The friend here seems loving. The friend here seems kind. The friend here is meeting the loner's needs, addressing Stearns' "hole" in the gospel. The friend here couldn't be *Satan*, could he?

The process of detecting satanic activity from true righteousness concerns the vital area of *spiritual discernment*. It is the ability to separate biblical truth from falsehood accurately and reliably. And without a doubt, the lack of spiritual discernment among professing Christians is *the* most neglected demand God makes upon believers in our day.

Discernment: The Neglected Imperative

Where does God command believers to exercise spiritual discernment? Perhaps a better question is, where doesn't He? The answer is Philemon. Of all the books in the New Testament, this letter of twenty-five verses is the only one in which there is no instruction for the believer to be on guard against falsehood. All remaining twenty-six books of the New Testament (and many of the Old Testament) exhort the believer, to a greater or lesser degree, to discern truth from falsehood and to act upon it. In fact, Second Peter and Jude are written explicitly for this purpose. A summary statement on the need for spiritual discernment comes in Christ's warning at the end of His Sermon on the Mount: "**Beware of false prophets, who come to you in sheep's clothing but inwardly are ravenous wolves**" (**Matt 7:15**).

Wow! There it is in plain language, from no less an expert than Jesus! This is the climax of Jesus' longest uninterrupted teaching in Scripture. Jesus could have focused on a number of other issues as He concluded His momentous sermon, but He chose spiritual discernment. Not only that, He warned His listeners that the threat to them was as if being attacked by a wolf! Jesus is implying here that the risk of spiritual death—*eternal destruction!*—weighs in the balance. With such clear instruction from God, how could this imperative escape the Church's notice? How could today's professing believers be so blind to this danger? The answer is three-fold:

Ignorance. Many professing believers today are ignorant of what God's Word has to say and how it is to be interpreted, especially in the area of spiritual discernment. Many are not instructed in the complete counsel of God (**Acts 20:27**), and so are ignorant of its demands upon them. In fact, because a number of modern evangelical churches are themselves pastored by wolves, the teaching these congregations hear will tiptoe around any explicit warning to be on guard against spiritual falsehood.

Difficulty. Detecting falsehood from truth is challenging. It requires an awareness of how Satan operates (**2 Cor 2:11**). It requires constant vigilance, knowing that Satan is ceaseless and relentless in seeking to devour the unwitting and naïve (**1 Pet 5:8**). And it requires insight into his typical guise and ploy, that he resembles not the comically devilish caricature he has gone to great lengths to propagate, but rather an **"angel of light,"** and that his demons resemble **"servants of righteousness"** (**2 Cor 11:13-15**). It has been said Satan would always rather slightly pervert the truth than utter a complete falsehood. He does his best work, not by attacking the Church, but by *joining* it. This is why the great 19th century preacher Charles Spurgeon once wrote that discernment is not telling right from wrong; it is telling right from *almost* right—an arduous task indeed, especially for the uninformed and disinterested.

Unpopular. Even when falsehood is discovered, it is rarely denounced. Why not? Because in today's evangelical morass, that is to be *unloving.* Rather than follow God's dictum to expose and denounce falsehood for what it is (**Eph 5:11; 2 Cor 10:5; Titus 1:9; 2:15; 2 Tim 4:1-5; Rev 2:2**), today's pattern heads 180-degrees in the opposite direction, sweeping aside any doctrinal differences in the "broad-minded" search for unity. The modern evangelical ecumenical drive redefines love as acceptance and kindness as the universal embrace of any and all ideas with even the slightest patina of "Christianese." All that is required for entrance into the club is to be earnest and agreeable. Small wonder, then, that those raising their hands to identify unbiblical ideas and their source are more often scolded than applauded. The dominant paradigm of today's Church finds it unkind and unloving to inspect the ideas of a would-be Christian leader or teacher, looking for any telltale seams in an otherwise congenial veneer that might uncover lupine intent.

Biblical Strategies for "Wolf Detection"

So how do we correct this disobedient drift? Supposing one wants to obey God's guidelines regarding the detection and denigration of falsehood, how does the believer exercise such biblical discernment? Christ's example in His confrontation with Satan gives us straightforward guidelines:

Read, study and apply God's Word. Jesus answers each of Satan's temptations with Scripture, quoting Deuteronomy every time in retort to the devil's lies (**Matt 4:1-10**). In doing so, He establishes the pattern for His true followers in their confrontations with Satan and his minions. Christians need to use the Word of God just as Jesus did, as a weapon for both defending the truth (**1 Pet 3:15**) and for tearing down falsehood (**2 Cor 10:3-5**). God describes His Word as a fire, a rock and a sword in destroying all forms of error (**Jer 23:29; Heb 4:12**). Christians must have a ready command for the martial use of God's Word against false doctrine, just as God intends.

Pray. Although **Matthew 4:1-2** does not explicitly mention that Jesus was praying, we can infer He did this along with His fast. Prayer and fasting are often linked in Scripture (**Dan 9:3; Luke 2:37; Acts 14:23**). Moreover, all other passages where Jesus goes to be alone mentions His praying (**Matt 14:23; Luke 5:16; 6:12; 9:28; Mark 1:35**).

Prayer helps the discernment-desiring believer in a number of ways. It brings him or her into a proper place of reverence, awe and humility before God, recognizing there is fearsomeness to His holiness and to His wrath against falsehood. It sharpens one's commitment to righteousness through repentance of encumbering sins so that one might be sober-minded and alert to falsehood. It invites the Holy Spirit to bring illumination of the Word and its uses against Satan. And it solicits the blessing of God for those wayward in their doctrine, that He might open their blind eyes and redirect them toward truth—the ultimate goal of any discernment ministry.

Test the spirits (**1 John 4:1**). What does this mean? It means to place what you are hearing, reading or witnessing from those professing like-minded faith alongside what God has put in His Word. Does it align? Does the would-be partner in faith know and embrace the gospel? Is he or she able to articulate it accurately and clearly as, "**the power of God for salvation to everyone who believes**" (**Rom 1:16**)? Or is it in some refurbished form focused more on earthly considerations and culturally approved values (we discuss this in greater detail in Chapters 4 and 5)? In His temptation, Jesus knew the Word of God so perfectly that He readily identified its violation in the wiles of Satan.

Differentiate a person from his/her ideas. The Bible says we are always to be ambassadors for people (**2 Cor 5:18-21**), even as we war for and against ideas (**2 Cor 10:5**). The Christian has only one enemy, Satan himself (**1 Pet 5:8**). His henchmen are not our ultimate enemies but rather candidates for salvation to whom we proclaim God's Word. As such, we need not fear the denunciation of falsehood as though it somehow endangers its proponent. After all, ideas are fungible. No one is inextricably connected to his or her own error, as though it is integral to his or her makeup. Part of the process of growing in the grace and knowledge of the Lord Jesus Christ—which all believers are to do (**2 Pet 3:18**)—involves the abandonment of error for truth. So do not recoil from the confident censure of a professing believer's error, provided it is done in love, gentleness and respect (**1 Cor 13:1-3; 2 Tim 2:24-26**). You are not undermining who he or she is as a person. On the contrary, you are opening him or her to the opportunity to exchange error for truth.

So how is your commitment to spiritual discernment? How sensitive is your antennae to the beckoning of Satan? Who are today's evangelical wolves? Can you recognize and name them readily?

The widespread and pervasive biblical exhortation to practice spiritual discernment is not an option for the believer. It is, rather, God's oft repeated and enduring command for those who would honor and glorify Him. With this in mind, let us commit ourselves to learning and applying

God's Word, to praying, to testing the spirits and to exercising godly wisdom as we, as Christ's sheep, persevere on the lookout for wolves.

3

Beware False Instruction
When the Sunday Sermon
Is Really Demon Doctrine

In the previous chapter, we introduced the believer's vital need for spiritual discernment in detecting teachers of truth from those who promote falsehood. Yet despite God's explicit warning, "...**in later times some will fall away from the faith, paying attention to deceitful spirits and doctrines of demons**" (**1 Tim 4:1**), many professing believers do just that. They proceed week to week exposed to noxious instruction that deftly yet decidedly unmoors them from the true Christian faith, blithely unaware of their predicament.

What are these "**doctrines of demons**" against which the Holy Spirit expressly warns? What is this toxic teaching that jeopardizes the faith of so many? The Apostle Paul provides a framework for its understanding in his critique of the church in Corinth: "**For if someone comes and proclaims *another Jesus* than the one we proclaimed, or if you receive a *different spirit* from the one you received, or if you** accept a *different gospel* from the one you accepted, you put up with it readily enough" (**2 Cor 11:4**; emphasis added).

This is the heart of the issue: a large swath of today's professing believers are regularly "putting up" with false teaching on Jesus, His Spirit, and His gospel, with nary a suspicion of harm, let alone any objection or pushback. They come expecting to be shown the narrow path to eternal life, when in fact they are being led down the wide road that leads to destruction (**Matt 7:13-14**). For this reason, **2 Corinthians 11:4** may be the most pertinent and yet underappreciated verse in the New Testament in our day, as the categories addressed by Paul remain the *three key pillars of demonic doctrine* plaguing the Church for the past two millennia.

"Another Jesus"

Demonic doctrines all have at their core a faulty view of Christ. Oh, their proponents may make all the right claims about Jesus and His divinity—that He is indeed the Son of God, who died and rose again for the sins of the world. They may endorse and uphold all the confessional statements, and dutifully insist their Christology is fully orthodox. They will prominently feature the name of Jesus in their teaching, and oversee philanthropic church ministries designed and promoted as being Jesus' contemporary "hands and feet." Their Jesus welcomes all who come to Him, helps those in need, exemplifies the humility by which we are to live, brings love to the outcast and highlights mercy in response to wrongs—just as the Bible declares.

But here's the rub: false teachers who bring "another Jesus" will inevitably exclude those aspects of the Bible's Jesus that don't align with their concept of who He should be. In particular, they will abridge, revise or (most likely) completely omit Jesus' instruction regarding coming judgment. They will ignore Jesus' emphatic warning to fear God, because not only can He kill, but also cast whom He has killed into hell (**Luke 12:4-5**). Their Jesus does not bring a sword instead of peace (**Matt 10:34**), require complete abandonment of all worldly relationships and affections as the price of salvation (**Luke 14:26**), and promise everlasting punishment to those who do not repent and believe (**Luke 13:1-5; John 3:18; 8:24; Matt 25:46**). At no time would their Jesus withhold His truth from anyone (**Matt 11:27; Mark 4:10-12**). In no way is their Jesus One who returns, ". . . **in flaming fire, inflicting vengeance on those who do not know God and on those who do not obey the gospel of our Lord Jesus**" (**2 Thess 1:8**). In no sense would He ever supervise the eternal suffering of rebels in hell (**Rev 14:10**).

"A Different Spirit"

When you get Jesus wrong, you inevitably get the Spirit wrong. Why is that? Because the Spirit to which Paul refers is the very Spirit of Christ, whose arrival was predicted by Jesus and timed with His Ascension (**John 16:7**). This is the same Spirit of Christ who inspired the perfect and inerrant Scriptures (**1 Pet 1:11**). He is the Spirit who begat (**Luke 1:35**), led (**Luke 4:1**), and empowered Christ throughout His ministry (**Luke 4:14**). He is the Spirit who regenerates and lives within those who repent and believe in Christ's atoning work (**Ezek 36:26-27; John 7:38-39; Rom 8:9**). And He is the Spirit who convicts the world, "**concerning sin and righteousness and judgment**" (**John 16:8**).

A false Christ thus yields a false spirit—the spirit of the age—and all the attendant errors that reliance upon this spirit brings, including (and perhaps most importantly) *invalid interpretation of Scripture*. How so? Because the true Spirit of Christ is He who guides the believer into all truth (**1 John 2:20, 27**). The Bible explicitly states that God's Spirit is necessary for one to know the "**deep things of God**," as found in His Word (**1 Cor 2:10-13**). So when a false spirit is substituted, then all bets are off when it comes to proper biblical understanding. Without the real Spirit of Christ to decode God's Word, all forms of spiritual delusion—though dressed up as faithful biblical instruction—are guaranteed to ensue.

Consequently, you will find those who represent demonic doctrines marked by continual reimagining of passages to suit their purposes (the theological term for this is *eisegesis*, as opposed to *exegesis*). These false teachers will eschew expository preaching as unhelpful or even as "too easy" and will consult and rely upon the spirit of the age to ensure that none of their pronouncements ever offend popular thinking.

"A Different Gospel"
Finally, those representing another Jesus and a different spirit will inevitably bring a different gospel. That such a false gospel can be foisted on those who have already believed and been saved astonished the Apostle Paul (**Gal 1:6-8; 3:1**) and should likewise astonish us. Why? Because the true gospel is the most important message of the Bible, and it is not at all veiled or obscure. Paul's definition of the gospel is both concise and unambiguous (**Rom 1:16**): "... **the power of God for salvation to everyone who believes**." The true gospel is all about salvation which comes to every sinner who, by the power of God, believes. Believes what? "**Christ died for our sins...He was buried...He was raised on the**

third day" (**1 Cor 15:3-4**). That could not be more simple or clear. Regrettably, the simple and clear biblical gospel is under such tremendous assault from enemy forces today that it lies tattered and barely recognizable in places long thought to be secure from any menace.

As an example, witness the dramatic rise of the "social justice" gospel and its co-opting of many within evangelical Christianity who should have seen it coming and known better than to acquiesce.[9] On what basis were they warned? Here's a hint: whenever the proposed gospel understanding is focused on present material conditions and earthly injustices and not spiritual condition and on the things to come (**2 Cor 4:17-18**), then you have found yourself exposed to "a different gospel."

The perpetual and distinguishing mark of any false gospel is the *addition of human effort*. This is the common denominator in all onslaughts against the true gospel. Several years ago, one influential mega-church pastor and popular author conceded to his congregation that, yes, the gospel involves the death and resurrection of Jesus Christ for the redemption of the world—he'd grant that is true. But, he added, *that wasn't all*. For him, as for many, the idea that God saves those who merely repent and trust in His Son's substitutionary atoning work seems too artless, or insufficiently reparative, or unacceptable to the surrounding culture to be everything God requires for eternal life (he contemptuously caricatured repentant faith as some sort of hypothetical "minimum entrance requirement," in response to which God is obliged to let the assenting into heaven). No, he insisted, there is more to it than that, and went on to emphasize his own

---

[9] The pernicious threat of "social justice" to the gospel of Jesus Christ is discussed further in chapters 4 and 5.

"gospel" as being what we do for God in response to what He has done for us.

In reality, the one true gospel is always and only a gospel of divine accomplishment—nothing less and nothing more. Any variations adding some form of human achievement to the mix are fabricated facsimiles ultimately deriving from Satan. The only obedience that ever merited any reward from God was the perfect obedience of Christ to the will of the Father (**Phil 2:8, 9**). No matter the particulars, whenever human activity is presented as a necessary contribution to the redemption represented by the true gospel, it becomes demonic doctrine. The Apostle Paul writes to those who would add their own merit alongside Christ's in God's plan of redemption: **"You are severed from Christ, you who would be justified by the law; you have fallen from grace"** (**Gal 5:4**). Seek to add your own work to that which Christ has done to save you, and you are doomed. That was true when Paul wrote Galatians, and it remains true today.

What's Behind Demon Doctrines?

Ultimately, these assaults against God's Word—presenting another Jesus, a different Spirit, and a different gospel—are aimed at one target: undermining the truth of God's Word. Since the Father seeks worshippers in truth (**John 4:23**), since Jesus is full of truth (**John 1:14**), came to bear witness to the truth (**John 18:37**), and in fact *is* the Truth (**John 14:6**), since the Spirit of Christ is the Spirit of truth (**John 15:26**), and since the gospel as found in God's Word is truth (**John 17:17**), what is clearly in the sights of Satan is *truth*. Truth is what matters most to God, which is why it is most assailed by His number one enemy. Why such a focused obsession? Because Satan knows if the truth of God's Word can be successfully undermined, then the only manner by which one might be saved (**Rom 10:17**) can be foiled. That has been Satan's strategy from the time his first temptation led to the first sin—"**Did God really say...?**" (**Gen 3:1**)—and it remains his *modus operandi* ever since.

Fortunately, God has promised that His truth will endure throughout the ages. As **Psalm 119:160** declares, "**The sum of Your Word is truth, and every one of your righteous rules endures forever.**" Meanwhile, knowing the final outcome is secure, true believers are entrenched in a battle with demon forces over God's truth. We are vying against the enemy's doctrines of demons and their core depictions— another Jesus, a different spirit and a different gospel—with the Word of truth God has spoken and now illuminates to those who are His. May God empower those who claim to be of this truth worthy for such a task.

4

Beware False Trends
"Social Justice" versus the Bible

Critical Race Theory. Intersectionality. Identity politics. Reparations. Wokeness. These ideas undergirding and framing the concept of "social justice"—so prominent in today's cultural discussion—have in recent times even infiltrated the Church and begun to take root. Today, many leading Christian voices are becoming susceptible to these ideas and are even seeking to reorient the Church's primary purpose and focus in these directions.

But is this right? What would Jesus think about this trend? As the "social justice" juggernaut continues to batter the breastwork of the Church, it would seem to be a propitious moment to look deeper into what the Head of the Church thinks about the issue. Does Scripture give any insight into the thoughts of Jesus regarding the "social justice" movement? The answer is an unmistakable "yes," and—to the likely surprise and consternation of those driving the "social justice" movement forward within the Church—His words should give them considerable pause.

Let's start with the obvious: Jesus does not oppose *justice*. On the contrary, Jesus is the Originator, Definer, Overseer and Executor of justice (**Matt 12:18, 20**). With regard to human interactions, the Bible uses the term "justice" to denote the condition of being impartial, even-handed, and scrupulous, and Jesus explicitly supports such an ethic (**Luke 11:42; 18:7-8; John 7:24**). Another manner by which justice is understood is moral perfection, and on that score, Jesus is the supreme example (**Ps 145:17**). Further, the biblical concept of justice ultimately contends that all its supplicants will get exactly what they are promised, and Jesus guarantees that He will be there at the end, making it so (**John 5:27-29; Rev 19:2**).

So if Jesus is the Author, Champion, Living Exemplar, and ultimate Enforcer of *all* justice, He *must* be in favor of "social justice"—right? To get an accurate biblical answer to this question, we must understand how the modifier compromises and corrupts the virtue. The Bible *never* uses any modifiers for "justice," let alone "social," which in itself should deter those who would speak and reason biblically from use of this term (for this reason, throughout this chapter the term "social justice" is set off in quotations, to indicate its illegitimacy as a biblical term and notion). But because the undiscerning Church seemingly cannot resist the appeal of "social justice," it is incumbent upon those who would claim to represent Jesus to understand and discuss its full portent.

For our purposes, we will use the following definition for "social justice:"

A philosophical and political concept holding that, because all people in this world should have equal access to wealth, health, opportunity and well-being, all people of this world are thus obliged to make it so.

You may ask, what's wrong with that? All for one and one for all in striving for equality? Why wouldn't the One who is ultimately bringing "**justice to victory**" (cf. **Isa 42:1-3; Matt 12:20**) support this effort? The Bible gives us *four compelling reasons* why He does not:

"Social Justice" Misapprehends the *Eschaton*

One text in Scripture giving particular insight into Christ's perspective on the matter of "social justice" is found in **Luke 12:13-15**. It reads:

> **Someone in the crowd said to Him, 'Teacher, tell my brother to divide the inheritance with me.' But He said to him, 'Man, who made Me a judge or arbiter over you?' And He said to them, "Take care, and be on your guard against all covetousness, for one's life does not consist in the abundance of his possessions."**

Here, Jesus is confronted by a man who has (in his opinion) been deprived of his fair share of an inheritance. From a "social justice" perspective, the man has been wronged, in that he believes he is owed wealth that has not been forthcoming. The man thus appeals to Jesus as an authority figure to find in his favor and correct the perceived injustice. This is a quintessential "social justice" scenario: resources have been appropriated in an asymmetric (therefore, unfair) manner, and the one deprived thus seeks redress.

But does Jesus give empathy and succor to the plaintiff? Does He commiserate with the aggrieved brother and come

51

to his aid? Quite the opposite. In fact, Jesus gives the man a curt rebuke! He begins by asking the man why He should be a judge or arbiter in this situation. This response should arouse our curiosity, because as the Bible makes clear, Jesus knows His Father has handed all judgment over to Him (**John 5:22, 27; 9:39**). His response to the man is therefore puzzling. After all, with all judgment handed over to Him, why wouldn't Jesus be the perfect judge in this, as in all, matters?

The answer is twofold. The first has to do with the *ordo eschaton*, the order of last things, or how the world is going to end according to the plan of God. Jesus is here giving a revealing (if indirect) eschatological lesson. Jesus knows full well His time for judgment is coming, when He will judge the entire world with perfect justice based upon the Word God has given (**John 12:48**). But He also knows from the fall of Jerusalem and the Babylonian Captivity (605 BC-586 BC) through His time upon the earth and right up to the present is described by God as, **"the times of the Gentiles"** (**Luke 21:24; Rom 11:25**). During this period of history, Jesus understands His Father's plan is not *judgment* but *salvation*. Yes, Jesus is the final Judge of this world, but this comes later. For now, God is still graciously saving sinners through the narrow door of repentance and faith. In His rhetorical query, then, Jesus is deferring present judgment of earthly matters. His desire is for the man to forego the redress of an alleged earthly injustice, and instead prepare his heart through repentance and faith in anticipation of the judgment that is to come.

Many evangelicals who pander to ideas of "social justice" operate from an erroneous postmillennial or theonomic eschatology. To their way of thinking, the earthly kingdom

Jesus is promised to bring (**2 Sam 7:12**) has already been inaugurated with His first appearance, and it is thus up to His followers to implement its form. And when one convolutes the Bible's prophecies regarding the present and future ages in this manner, the fallout is a naturally erroneous fixation on the redress and reparation of inequalities in the here and now. But that is not what the Bible says about God's intent in the present, nor in the future. God will indeed bring to fruition the promised earthly kingdom of Christ (**Rev 20:1-6**), but He will do it without need of any human partnership (**Acts 17:25**), and only when the sum of those who are appointed to eternal life believe (**Acts 13:48**). For now, Jesus as Judge and Arbiter of the world is on hold, being mercifully delayed, **"until the fullness of the Gentiles has come in"** (**Rom 11:25**). Jesus' just judgment of the world is coming, but—in God's inexplicable and extraordinary love, mercy and grace— He continues to delay that day, such that **"now is the day of salvation"** (**2 Cor 6:2; 2 Pet 3:9**).

"Social Justice" Often Arises From Sinful Impulse

The second reason why Jesus defers to judge in this man's case is found in the continuation of Jesus' remarks to the crowd: **"And He said to them, 'Take care, and be on your guard against all covetousness, for one's life does not consist in the abundance of his possessions'"** (**Luke 12:15**). Here, Jesus unambiguously ties concern over earthly inequalities with the potential for sin—*the sin of covetousness*. And His implication is blunt: the focus upon earthly inequalities, even with the intent of their amelioration, *by its very nature* introduces the possibility of covetousness. Jesus is saying that those obsessed with rectifying worldly inequalities as they pertain to themselves should first reflect about a possible covetous impulse.

James then elaborates on this idea:

> **What causes quarrels and what causes fights among you? Is it not this, that your passions are at war within you? You desire and do not have, so you murder. You covet and cannot obtain, so you fight and quarrel . . . You adulterous people! Do you not know that friendship with the world is enmity with God? Therefore, whoever wishes to be a friend of the world makes himself an enemy with God (James 4:1-2, 4-5).**

So, Jesus claims that those obsessing over their unfair or unequal treatment in this world must guard against covetousness, and the Spirit through James says covetousness lies at the core of fights and quarrels as to who has what and who does not. This link is no mere coincidence. The rancor and invectives that so often attend plaintiff demands for "social justice" lie in stark contrast to the fruits of the Spirit-led life, as laid out in **Galatians 5:22-23**, and this passage in James identifies the core reason for this. The Bible is clear: whenever there is a focus upon remediation of earthly inequality, covetousness may very well lie at the source, and when it does, acrimony and outrage are the typical byproduct.

In addition, note how the Spirit through James goes on to associate covetousness with friendship with the world. This also is no coincidence. Not only do the evangelical champions of "social justice" often carry with them a misguided eschatology, but also quite commonly a penchant for the favor of the world. In fact, when one looks out over the sea of modern evangelicalism to those at the helm of the S.S. Social Justice, one finds a remarkably common deference to culture and desire for its approval. Today's most prominent evangelical crusaders for "social justice" almost always seem to be those most eager to be received well by the secular procurators of modern-day politics, academia, business and social media, and this passage from James helps to explain why.

"Social justice" Misconstrues Human Nature and its Fundamental Need

There is a third reason Jesus opposes "social justice," and that is its failure to apprehend the Bible's description of human nature. In **Luke 19:10**, Jesus declares, "**For the Son of Man came to seek and to save the lost.**" And who are the lost? Jesus' answer is clear: they are the spiritually "**harassed and helpless, like sheep without a shepherd**" (**Matt 9:36; Mark 6:34**). They are the spiritually poor prisoners, blind and oppressed (**Matt 5:3; Luke 4:18**). And from the days of the early Church until recently, it has been understood that the manner by which Jesus saves the *spiritually* lost is through gospel evangelism by those whom He has already *spiritually* saved.

But all this is now being challenged on the evangelical "social justice" front. No longer are the "lost" being defined on a spiritual basis, but on economic and/or sociological terms. And no longer is the manner by which Jesus saves the "lost" through a call to "**repentance and the forgiveness of sins**" (**Luke 24:47**), but rather through His purported desire that earthly injustices be remedied, including (and perhaps preferably) through governmental policies and programs. This is exactly how neo-Marxist dogma is now being foisted upon an unsuspecting Church under the guise of "social justice."

A natural corollary of this development is that those to be involved in "evangelism" no longer must be "born again" in a "saved from sin" sense. Rather, they must merely exhibit interest in bettering the material and social conditions of the disadvantaged around them. Whereas in the past, people were required to "believe in order to belong," it is somehow suggested that now they might "belong" regardless of belief. But Jesus knows the heart of the unredeemed is, **"deceitful above all things and desperately sick"** (**Jer 17:9**), that the mind of the unredeemed is, **"darkened in** [its] **understanding, alienated from the life of God because of the ignorance that is in them"** (**Eph 4:18**), and that the will of the unredeemed is to, **"do their father's** [the devil's] **desires"** (**John 8:44**). Given all that, Jesus knows that the real need of the unregenerate sinner—regardless of race, wealth, or any other earthly designation—is heart, mind and will *transformation* via **"repentance and the forgiveness of sins"** (**Luke 24:47**); in a word—*salvation*. Not only that, given that salvation only comes from belief, under no circumstances could an unbeliever ever contribute in a positive sense to the saving work God is doing in the world today.

One passage plainly detailing the above is **John 7:38-39**, where Jesus declares: **"Whoever believes in me, as the Scripture has said, 'Out of his heart will flow rivers of living water.' Now this he said about the Spirit, whom those who *believed* in him were to receive, for as yet the Spirit had not been given, because Jesus was not yet glorified"** (emphasis added). Here, **"rivers of living water"** is participation in God's work in the world, about which Jesus stipulates the following: penitent belief yields the indwelling

Spirit, which in turn yields power for the spiritual work God is doing. *Only in that order.* One's *position* in Christ establishes one's *practice* for Christ, and never the reverse.[10] Given this, how then could Jesus back a movement that obsesses over the material and/or sociological condition of the sinner but cares little for how that sinner might be forgiven and granted eternal life?

The condition of the unredeemed is described in the Bible (**Rom 8:5-12**) as living "**in the flesh,**" about which it makes the following clear and unambiguous designation (**Rom 8:8**): "**Those who are in the flesh cannot please God.**" *Ever.* It is a travesty of Christ's teaching that a church could lead its members in works of "social justice" without telling them of their need to be redeemed, and how this might be accomplished. It is a travesty of Christ's teaching that a collection of earnest but unredeemed "Jesus-followers" might pursue good works to assist the disadvantaged, while at the same time have no clue as to how both they and those whom they serve might be saved from their sin.

"Social Justice" Conflicts with the Church's True Task

A final and related reason Jesus opposes "social justice" is that it directly undermines the primary task of the Church. To see this, one must understand the overarching purpose of the Church is to declare God's Word, and that the summary goal of all biblical instruction is the following: to present God's righteous standard to all sinners (**Matt 5:48**), to drive those sinners to despair at their inability to attain the righteousness

---

[10] John MacArthur, "The Body Formed in Eternity Past, Part 2," Grace Community Church, Sun Valley, CA, Jan. 15, 1978.
https://www.gty.org/library/sermons-library/1903/the-body-formed-in-eternity-past-part-2

demanded of them by a holy God (**Lev 11:44-45; Gal 3:10-11, 19-24**), to have those sinners cry out for mercy to that same gracious God for a pardon from their sin (**Luke 18:13-14**), and to have faith that God will, as promised, apply to them the righteousness of Christ, who lovingly bore their sins upon the cross (**Isa 53:10-11; 2 Cor 5:21**). That is the crux of the gospel, *the* paramount message of the Church, and notice it hinges upon a requisite contrite spirit (**Isa 57:15**).

But when the Church reorients its focus to concerns regarding "social justice," it short-circuits and inverts this entire process. No longer is the sinner a perpetrator; now he or she is a victim. No longer does the sinner plead for mercy to a gracious and forgiving God; now he or she is owed something from Him, or at least from the world He oversees. No longer are sinners "**poor in spirit**" and thus eligible for the kingdom of God (**Matt 5:3**). Now they are casualties of tyrannical forces that exploit and subjugate them in a bondage of oppression, against which they must rage until scores are settled. The upshot? Instead of sinners acknowledging and repenting of their sinful condition, they are now emboldened to seek recourse against as many injustices as they can identify. Gone is the meek and humble spirit that ultimately inherits the earth (**Ps. 37:5; Matt 5:5**). In its place is a spirit of victimization, rebellion and retribution.

It is for this reason that, across the landscape of modern-day evangelicalism, one tends to find an inverse relationship between interest in "social justice" and interest in evangelism in its historic understanding. In a very real sense, the entire mission of the Church is being hijacked. Among those on the evangelical forefront of the "social justice" movement, the talk is no longer about how sinners might avoid eternal damnation in hell, but how they might gain temporal reparation for past and present injustices.

"Social justice" carries with it the implicit idea the sinner in this world is owed something by someone, but that idea is completely foreign to Jesus. Even among His redeemed, Jesus claims they are owed nothing in this world:

> **Will any one of you who has a servant plowing or keeping sheep say to him when he has come in from the field, 'Come at once and recline at table'? Will he not rather say to him, 'Prepare supper for me, and dress properly, and serve me while I eat and drink, and afterward you will eat and drink?' Does he thank the servant because he did what was commanded? So you also, when you have done all that you were commanded, say, "We are unworthy servants; we have only done what was our duty" (Luke 17:7-10).**

Jesus' point is clear: if even those who are a part of His kingdom are mere "servants," with no rights nor entitlements other than to consider themselves as ever-unworthy and thus duty-bound to their Master, how much more so would this apply to those on the outside looking in?

It has been written elsewhere that if the parable of the Prodigal Son had been set in the age of "social justice," the son would have never returned home to his Father. And why should he have? Once apprised that he was not an ungrateful, impudent, hedonistic fool in need of repentance and humble submission to his Father, but rather a victim of external, impersonal, malevolent forces stemming from unfair societal arrangements, his path would have led not to the true home of his Father's embrace and promise of eternal life, but rather to the false embrace of "social justice" promising entitlements to dampen his fall. Gone would be any notion of regret or remorse at his sin. In its place, as a result of his "social justice" reeducation? Only resentment, indignation, and perpetual rebellion.

Conclusion: What Does Jesus Offer?

With the biblical record so consistently opposed to the *zeitgeist* of "social justice," it should appall the Church that it could be so easily and so harmfully beguiled as it has been. Jesus offers the sinner not a list of earthly entitlements to be pursued and defended at all costs, but rather inexplicable love and mercies despite that same sinner's enmity (**Lam 3:22-23; Rom 5:8,10; 8:8**). Jesus doesn't offer the sinner the right to claim victimhood and redress against earthly injustices, but only the right to claim eternal unworthiness for His promise of eternal life. The Church is called not to a mission of political and economic lobbying for the betterment of this world, but a mission calling sinners to repentance for their betterment in the next (**Luke 5:32**). As to worldly arrangements and the material goals of "social justice" devotees, Jesus asks, "**What will it profit a man if he gains the whole world and forfeits his soul**" (Matt 16:26)? May God raise up within His Church those who know the answer to this question, and from that answer might clarify the true gospel from its "social justice" corruption.

5

Beware False Trends II
What's Behind the "Social Justice" Gospel-ers?

In September, 2018, a collection of concerned pastors and theologians forged a document entitled, "A Statement on Social Justice and the Gospel" (sometimes also known as the "Dallas Statement").[11] Crafted around fourteen distinct affirmations and denials, its *raison d'etre* is set forth in its opening statement: "In view of questionable sociological, psychological, and political theories presently permeating our culture and making inroads into Christ's church, we wish to clarify certain key Christian doctrines and ethical principles prescribed in God's Word. Clarity on these issues will fortify believers and churches to withstand an onslaught of dangerous and false teachings that threaten the gospel, misrepresent Scripture, and lead people away from the grace of God in Jesus Christ." The statement's biblical foundation

---

[11] The entire statement can be found at
https://statementonsocialjustice.com/

is so rigorous, not even those most opposed to the statement's conception can disagree with its content. As such, it is helping to serve as a firewall against an onslaught of theological deviancies presently having their heyday within modern evangelicalism around the subject of "social justice."

But even as this latest assault on God's doctrine of salvation is confronted, the struggle should trigger a remembrance in every thoughtful Christian's mind. It is a lesson reinforced repeatedly by the cyclical rhythm of church history, as follows: *When one merges human amelioration of suffering and injustice with divine remediation of sin, inevitably the purpose and impact of the cross and resurrection of Jesus Christ takes a backseat.* This is the sad legacy of mainline Protestant denominations over the past century—a rise in the focus on enhancing social welfare tightly correlated with a decline of interest in (and understanding of) how sinners might be saved from their sin.

The Incomparable True Gospel

So how does the "social justice" gospel maintain its appeal? To elaborate, how could the *evangelion* of Jesus Christ, with its transcendent promises—that a sinner worthy only of eternal punishment can be forgiven of all moral debt (**Col 2:13-14; 1 John 1:9**), can be robed in the righteousness of the Savior (**Isa 61:10**), can be adopted by God as a full-fledged sibling of Christ (**Rom 8:15-17**), can be set higher than angelic beings with the same glory as of God Himself (**John 1:12; 1 Cor 6:3; 1 John 3:2**), and can be made an ambassador of Christ for the sake of other souls He seeks to save (**2 Cor 5:18-20**)—how could such an infinite, too-marvelous-for-words opportunity ever be pedestrianized with finite goals such as elimination of economic disparities and redress of earthly inequalities? With such a stupendous opportunity at stake, why would anyone be tempted to substitute *anything* for the incomparable prize of the upward call (**Phil 3:14**)?

Jesus knew how ludicrous any conflation of earthly and heavenly possibilities would be, asking—incredulously—, **"For what does it profit a man to gain the whole world and forfeit his soul?"** (**Mark 8:36**). For Jesus, it does not matter how much one might improve his or her condition in this world—even to the conquest of it all!—if such a development also brought eternal damnation. In another passage, Jesus wonders why one would come to Him to remediate an earthly injustice when His heavenly offer beckons, even (as we saw in the last chapter) going so far as to implicate covetousness as the root cause of fixation on earthly conditions (**Luke 12:13-15**).

The true gospel is about how penitent and believing sinners—no matter the race, nationality, gender, or any other category—*forfeit the world in becoming united in one spiritual family* (**Eph 2:13-22**). They do this precisely because a Holy Father has redeemed them through faith in the substitutionary work of the Holy Son. It is about how one turns his or her back on the temporal in order to have one's sins forgiven, blotted out and remembered no more (**Isa 43:25; Heb 8:12**). It is about renunciation of this world and all its attractions for the sake of an eternal inheritance that is, **"imperishable, undefiled, and unfading, kept in heaven for you"** (**1 Pet 1:4**). It is about how doing the above grants access to the throne room of God! (**Rom 5:1-2**). This should not be a tough sell, folks.

So, given all of the above, given the gulf between what God offers in His true gospel and what "social justice" gospel-ers are offering in theirs, how does their so-called "social justice" gospel maintain any traction? What's behind

63

the "social justice" gospel-ers and their incessant focus on the temporal and material, on the evanescent here and now?

Biblical Christianity: Benevolent Works *and* Benevolent Words

The Bible is not silent on this question. In fact, it provides a universal explanation behind all corruptions of the true gospel, regardless of the age or form. But before we explore God's explanation behind "social justice" (or any other) distortions of the true gospel, we must first address the *two distinct aspects* of what it means to be a Christian: (1) what one does and (2) what one says. From the earliest days of the Church, these have always been the twin features of the authentic Christian life. We might term them the *benevolent works* and *benevolent words* of the faithful.

Let's start with benevolent works, i.e. what one does as a Christian. The Bible is clear—Christians love (**1 Cor 13:35**). They serve (**John 13:14-15**). They bind up the wounds of the hurting, feed the hungry, and clothe the poor (**Isa 58:10**). They remember the widows and orphans and others who are easily forgotten (**Isa 1:17; James 1:27**). They care for the stranger, for the sick, and for the imprisoned (**Matt 25:34-40**). And do you know what? *The world loves it all.* Write it down: the world has always esteemed the good works of Christians. In fact, it will even seek to partner with Christians in doing these works. The conflict between the world and the Christian promised by Jesus (**John 7:7; 15:18; 16:1-4; 1 John 2:15-17**) never comes from the world's disapproval of the benevolent *works* of the Christian.

No, the conflict between the world and the Christian comes only in the other aspect of what it means to be a Christian, when the faithful believer proclaims the benevolent words of salvation. Here is where the love affair between the world and the real Jesus abruptly ends. Why is that? Because as much as the world will love what Christians *do*, when those same Christians are faithful in proclaiming the true gospel of Jesus Christ, the world will hate what they have to *say* (**Matt 10:22; Luke 21:17; John 15:19**).

Christians do good works and enjoy the affirmation of the world. Then the faithful open their mouths, starting with the announcement of a holy God who cannot look upon evil (**Hab 1:13**), and who has promised its eventual just judgment (**Eccl 12:14**). They tell the world that evil is endemic to all as the result of Adam's fall, and therefore everyone lives under a sentence of condemnation and coming judgment (**John 3:18; 36**). The faithful plead with the world to repent before Christ the Savior and surrender to His Lordship (**Mark 1:15**). The faithful warn all who will listen that apart from repentance and belief in the transforming work of Christ, they will die and spend eternity in hell as a penalty for their sin (**Ezek 18:4,20; Luke 13:1-5; John 8:24**). All the while, faithful Christians announce the true gospel—the "good news"—that God will forgive those who repent and trust in His grace to pardon them of their sin, knowing that the true gospel message is the only hope for sinners. And because the gospel they proclaim is the only hope for a dying world, faithful Christians know that pointing sinners to the eternal life God offers for those who repent and believe is *true love*.

Biblical Christianity: The Example of Jesus

But the sinful, rebellious heart is wired such that, apart from God's effectual call and power to illuminate His truth, it spurns the benevolent words spoken by Christians. In fact, **Romans 1:18** says that the unrighteous suppress the truth *precisely because of their unrighteousness.* The last week of Jesus' life is a case study of the world's diametrically opposite responses to Christ's benevolent works and to His benevolent words. At the beginning of the week, Jesus rides into Jerusalem to the welcome of the adoring multitude, who hail Him as their coming King. The crowd had witnessed His miracles. They had eaten the miraculous loaves and fish (**John 6:1-14**). They had seen Lazarus raised from the dead (**John 11:1-44**). Jesus had proven to them with His miraculous works that He was someone of power and authority. The crowd worshipped Him for His signs, and they always pressured Him for more (**Matt 12:38; 16:1; Mark 8:11; Luke 11:29**).

So as Jesus rides into Jerusalem at the start of Passover Week, the people go before Him and cry, "Hosanna! Hosanna!" They are ready to follow Him as their leader. They are ready for the revolution and the new Kingdom they believe Jesus is introducing (cf. **Matt 21:1-11; Mark 11:1-11; Luke 19:28-40; John 12:12-15**). But do you notice that adoration does not last for long? In the following days, one sees Jesus deconstructing all the empty religious premises the people held dearest. One sees Him overturning the tables of profiteers in the temple and driving out the moneychangers (**Matt 21:12-13; Mark 11:15-19; Luke 19:45-48**). One sees Him undermining the Jews' entire form of religion as He upbraids their religious leaders (**Matt 23:1-36**). Pretty soon, the crowd has lost all its regard for Him. Now, Jesus is *saying* things *to* them, not *doing* things *for* them. And what He is saying insults them. His message offends them.

In a parable, He says that the owner (understood as God) of a vineyard (understood as Israel) is coming to destroy the tenants and give the vineyard to those who will be more faithful (**Matt 21:33-46; Mark 12:1-12**). The crowd knows that Jesus is referring to them as the unworthy tenants. So even though they cheered His entry into the city earlier in the week, by Friday they are crying, "Crucify Him! Crucify Him!" The benevolent *works* of Jesus brought the praise of the people. And, in the same manner, the benevolent *words* of Jesus brought about His crucifixion. The people loved His works and hated His words. And twenty-one centuries later, nothing has changed. God continues to bring sinners to repentance, day by day, one sinner at a time. But most ultimately reject His offer of eternal life, because they hate the message that they are sinners in need of a Savior.

Jesus says in **John 3:19**, "**And this is the judgment: the light has come into the world, and people loved the darkness rather than the light because their works were evil.**" Because the world loves its sin, the gospel message proclaimed by faithful Christians will provoke the world's hatred and rejection. And if one persists in declaring the benevolent message of pardon for repentance, it will ultimately bring persecution. Paul writes in **2 Timothy 3:12** that, "**... all who desire to live a godly life in Christ Jesus will be persecuted.**" This is the normal response to be anticipated for all faithful believers, for all who bring the true gospel message. The world has no problem with the Church doing good works. In fact, it welcomes them. It will even seek to partner with the Church in pursuing them. But the world despises the true message of the Church, the only message offering real hope by calling all to repentance and faith in Christ's atoning work. And it will reject and persecute those churches that persist in proclaiming the true gospel.

The Heart of the "Social Justice" Gospel: Persecution Avoidance

So here is our answer to the question posed in our title: *the social justice gospel is, at its core, generally driven by a desire to avoid repudiation by the world.* Do you doubt this? Then look and see the extent to which those propounding a "social justice" gospel have in their teaching and ministries any statements or positions that would incite the world's opprobrium. Go to the body of teaching of any prominent spokesperson for a "social justice" gospel and see how often that individual highlights the vilification and persecution God says will come to those who faithfully pursue His true gospel. Look hard and look long, because the examples will be slow in forthcoming.

Paul writes to the Galatians, **"It is those who want to make a good showing in the flesh who would force you to be circumcised, and only in order that they may not be persecuted for the cross of Christ"** (**Gal 6:12**). The Judaizers of Paul's day demanded that converts to Christianity must also comply with Jewish ceremonial stipulations—including circumcision—in order to be truly redeemed. The reason? The very real possibility that failing to comply with Jewish ordinances might lead to Roman persecution (**Acts 18:12-17**). This threat of persecution has attended all true gospel proclamation until now. From the days of the early Church, no matter the particulars of the age or threat, the rationale for deviation from the true gospel has always been fear of rejection, fear of reproach, fear of recrimination from a hostile world.

All false gospel efforts—including the "social justice" gospel—are attempts to have it both ways, to maintain a veneer of Christian orthodoxy while at the same time currying favor with the world. And what is the upshot? A reinvention of Jesus into someone who is less polarizing and more genteel, and a sanitization of His gospel into one that the world might find acceptable. But this is nothing less than apostasy. Do you ever wonder what God considers an apostate church? It is a church that is all about good *works*, and timidly avoids saving *words*. It is a church that aligns its ministry with the works the world wants to see—helping the poor, healing the sick, feeding the hungry—without simultaneously proclaiming the saving gospel the world despises. And as it pursues good works, even claiming to do them in Jesus' name, the apostate church will deliberately shun Jesus' saving words. Its distorted gospel—devoid of a biblical understanding of sin, divine judgment, repentance and saving faith—becomes, "God loves us, so let's love Him back by doing good works in the name of Jesus." It will avoid bold proclamation of the true gospel message, because the true gospel is a message that the world abhors, and the apostate church is ever genuflecting at the world's throne.

On the other hand, a true church knows that persecution is coming, but still remains faithful to the biblical gospel. A true church carefully extricates ideas of human munificence from the true gospel of divine accomplishment. A true church instructs its members on the two essential duties of all who are saved: yes—certainly! —benevolent *works* bringing temporal reprieve toward those deprived of justice or suffering from want. But these works, no matter how good and how necessary, are never to be elevated above—*and therefore lead to the exclusion of*—benevolent *words* bringing opportunity for redemption and eternal glory in union with God.

6

Beware False Assurance
On the Modern Day Assault Against the Dress Code of Heaven

What does it take to be right with God? That is the central question of human existence. What is God's criterion for eternal life with Him? What does He require?

Job had this question on his mind. The Book of Job is likely the oldest book in the Bible, so it is fitting that in it Job asks *the* question the Bible is written to answer: **"How then can man be in the right before God?"** (**Job 25:4; also 4:17; 9:2**). The correct answer determines the fate of everyone for all time. And because this is so, the correct answer is not only the most pondered and debated topic by humans, it is also the most undermined and attacked by God's number one enemy, Satan.

God's Perfect Standard
So what is the Bible's answer to this most fundamental question? What is God's demand upon those who would be received by Him? Answer: *perfection*. God's bar for His approval is perfection. Anything less brings eternal

condemnation as the price of disobedience. Ezekiel writes what God has determined: **"The soul that sins shall die"** (**Ezek 18:4, 20**).

This is God's consistent standard throughout Scripture. When God created the first humans, Adam and Eve, His instruction to them was straightforward: if you disobey Me, you will die (cf. **Gen 2:17**). When God delivered His Law to the people of Israel, His oft-repeated injunction—**"Be holy, for I am holy"** (**Lev 11:44-45; 19:2; 20:7**)—remained the same. And what was God's warning for all who fail in this? **"Cursed be anyone who does not confirm the words of this law by doing them"** (**Deut 27:26**). *Be perfect, or be cursed.* Those have always been God's two options.

This righteous standard was on David's heart when the Holy Spirit inspired him to write, **"O LORD, who shall sojourn in your tent? Who shall dwell on your holy hill? He who walks blamelessly and does what is right and speaks with truth in his heart"** (**Ps 15:1-2**). In another Psalm, David continues on this theme: **"Who shall ascend the hill of the LORD? And who shall stand in His holy place? He who has clean hands and a pure heart, and does not lift up his soul to what is false and does not swear deceitfully"** (**Ps 24:3-4**). And when God came to earth in the Person of Jesus Christ, His condition for acceptance was unchanged and explicit: **"You therefore must be perfect, as your heavenly Father is perfect"** (**Matt 5:48**). Earlier in the same sermon, Jesus warns those who would listen, **"For I tell you, unless your righteousness exceeds that of the scribes and Pharisees, you will never enter the kingdom of heaven"** (**Matt 5:20**).

So the standard of God for those who would commune with Him is consistent throughout Scripture and unequivocally clear: *holiness*. Moral perfection. A life lived flawlessly before God, free from even the slightest taint of sin. That is the Bible's daunting yet unambiguous requirement for fellowship and eternal life with God. And if that isn't enough, the Bible dooms its reader even further, declaring that on one's own, such perfection is impossible. According to the Bible, no one can live in such a manner, in perfect obedience before a righteous and holy God. David laments, **"No one living is righteous before you"** (**Ps. 143:2**). And in the New Testament, Paul concurs when he writes, **". . . all have sinned and fall short of the glory of God"** (**Rom 3:23a**). Therein lies the fundamental predicament of mankind: God demands holiness to match His glory, and everyone throughout all time falls short of this standard.

Imputation: God's "Robe of Perfection" Applied to Penitent Sinners

Most fortunately, God has provided a manner by which sinners can acquire the holiness necessary to commune with Him: through the *imputation* of Christ's righteousness to those who repent and believe in His saving work. Imputation means the transfer of condition from one account to another—in this case, the transfer of Christ's perfection to the unworthy. This imputation comes from God's provision of *penal substitutionary atonement*, wherein through faith God attributes the righteous life of Christ to the penitent sinner, and places that sinner's sins upon Christ, for which He was punished once and for all time upon the cross (**Isa 53:10; 2 Cor 5:21**). This is exactly what Isaiah was expressing when he says of Christ, **". . . by His knowledge shall the Righteous One, My Servant, make many to be accounted righteous, and he shall bear their iniquities"** (**Isa 53:11**).

The Bible uses a number of images to depict all that occurs in redeeming the sinner via imputation through substitutionary atonement, including speaking of being *clothed with the righteousness of God* (**Job 29:14**; italics added). The prophet Isaiah was beside himself at this possibility, exclaiming, "**I will rejoice greatly in the LORD, My soul will exult in my God; For He has clothed me with *garments of salvation*, He has wrapped me with a *robe of righteousness*"** (**Isa 61:10**; emphasis added). Zechariah elaborates on this sartorial makeover: "**He [God] spoke and said to those who were standing before him, saying, 'Remove the *filthy garments* from him.' Again He said to him, 'See, I have taken your iniquity away from you and will clothe you with *festal robes*'**" (**Zech 3:4**; italics added). In His revelation to the Apostle John, Jesus directly ties acquisition of cleansed robes with the sinner's right to enter heaven and enjoy eternal life with God (**Rev 22:14;** see also **7:14-17**).

This transfer of Christ's righteousness to sinners—pictured as a holy robe, given in exchange for their sinful soiled garment—is the most extraordinary transaction imaginable. It is almost beyond our ability to conceive that God would punish His own Son for the sins of others in order to provide this holy vestment, by which the sinner can stand perfectly righteous—and thus *accepted*—in the presence of God (**Rom 5:1-2; 8:1**). Substitutionary atonement and its provision of a righteous robe to unworthy sinners is thus the pinnacle demonstration of God's grace and mercy and love. As such, it is the supreme feature for which He deserves their highest and ceaseless praise.

But the prideful human heart is wired to reject God's offer of Christ's righteous robe, and instead to devise one of its own. Ever since Adam and Eve made garments of leaves in the vain attempt to cover the shame brought on by their sin, it has been mankind's nature to reject the covering God would apply, and endeavor instead to apply an alternative. This, in fact, is the impetus behind every false religion. Every false form of belief in the world is predicated, at its core, upon developing some alternative garment that might cover the sin and shame of its converts and somehow still allow them to stand acceptable before God.

Here is how one insightful pastor describes this tendency:

> What did Adam and Eve do? "**They sewed fig leaves together and made themselves loin coverings**" (**Gen 3:7**). That is the launch of false religion . . . that is the symbol of false religion. That is the first act of man to create a way in which he himself could deal with his own shame, in which he could cover his own iniquity. And then he hides, because he hasn't yet found a way to face God.
>
> This is the birth of false religion: men make ways to cover their own sin. But it does not salve their guilty conscience, and so they hide from God. False religion is a form of hiding from God, hiding from His true presence. That is the symbol of all false religion, that a guilty, dying sinner can make a covering for his own shame, and that somehow he can cover his shame and hide himself

from God. He hides himself in his own self-made coverings.[12]

Isaiah confirms the futility of these efforts: "**For all of us have become like one who is unclean, and all our righteous deeds are like a filthy garment; and all of us wither like a leaf, and our iniquities, like the wind, take us away**" (**Isa 64:6**). According to the prophet, these "**righteous deeds**" not only fail to cover one's sins and deliver the righteousness God requires, but are actually squalid waste which testify of the sinner's unrighteous core and augur his demise. It is for this reason **Proverbs 15:8** declares, "**The sacrifice of the wicked is an abomination to the LORD, but the prayer of the upright is acceptable to Him.**" And who are the wicked? *Everyone* who has not yet been made "**upright**" by the application of Christ's righteous robe. Although the rebellious heart of sinners yearns for any mode of spiritual dress other than the one stipulated by God, the Bible makes clear that all such endeavors are vain, despicable and worthless substitutes.

With such straightforward and consistent biblical instruction on God's righteous standard for acceptance, the gracious and singular manner He has arranged for this to occur, and the failure of all substituted human effort, one might think God's prescription for His approval would be immune to dispute. But if that is your conclusion, *guess again.*

God's Dress Code Under Attack

Now, we might expect those who reject outright the God of the Bible to formulate their own manner of acceptable dress

---

[12] John MacArthur, from the sermon, "The Danger of Adding to the Gospel: Gal 2:11-12," Grace Community Church, Sun Valley, CA, June 4, 2017.

before God—as it were, to clothe themselves in their own "righteous" works. But are you aware that God's singular manner of reconciling believing sinners by applying to them Christ's righteous robe is under attack *from within the church as well?* N.T. Wright—a darling among the revisionist evangelical set—has lead this attack in recent years. His so-called "New Perspective" on the gospel seeks to undermine the traditional, orthodox understanding of God's plan of salvation in several ways, including his claim that God never meant that Christ's righteousness could somehow be imputed to sinners. Wright is derisive of such an idea, claiming this doctrine is a misunderstanding of the gospel. He writes, "In certain circles within the church . . . 'the gospel' is supposed to be a description of how people get saved; of the theological mechanism whereby, in some people's language, Christ takes our sin and we his righteousness."[13]

Wright is insistent that this traditional Reformed understanding of the gospel involving penal substitutionary atonement has it all wrong. "This is not the gospel," he writes in his book *The Day the Revolution Began.* "This is paganism. To worship God as one who justifies by imputation is nonsense."[14] So as to leave no question on his denial of penal substitutionary atonement, he adds: "That Christ died in the place of sinners is closer to the pagan idea of an angry deity being pacified by a human death than it is to anything in either Israel's Scriptures or the New Testament."[15]

---

[13] N.T. Wright, *What Saint Paul Really Said: Was Paul of Tarsus the Real Founder of Christianity?* (Grand Rapids: Eerdmans, 1997), 39.

[14] N.T. Wright, *The Day the Revolution Began: Reconsidering the Meaning of Jesus' Crucifixion* (New York: Harper One, 2017), 147.

[15] Wright, *The Day the Revolution Began,* 147.

Elsewhere he writes:

> If we use the language of the law court, it makes no sense whatsoever to say that the judge imputes, imparts, bequeaths, conveys, or otherwise transfers his righteousness to either the plaintiff or the defendant. Righteousness is not an object, a substance, or a gas which can be passed across the courtroom. This gives the impression of a legal transaction, a cold piece of business, almost a trick of thought performed by a God who is logical and correct, but hardly one we want to worship.[16]

And what is his alternative? Wright contends that no one is justified—in other words, declared righteous by God—until one's final, future assessment. At that time—according to Wright—what the Apostle Paul meant as present justification by faith will be affirmed or denied on the basis of one's entire life.[17] Wright speaks of a person's "covenant faithfulness," wherein one maintains membership in God's covenant with His followers through vocational means (i.e. through obedience to His teaching), and anticipates a final justification at the end of time based at least partly in these obedient works. As Phil Johnson has remarked, this makes a person's faithful discipleship a factor in final justification. In other words, Wright's theology would ground ultimate salvation at least partly in the believer's activity while on Earth (Wright describes this as the "covenant of vocation"), and not

---

[16] Wright, *What Saint Paul Really Said*, 113.
[17] Wright, *What Saint Paul Really Said*, 129.

completely in the finished work of Christ on the sinner's behalf.[18]

Wright's purpose is to re-envision the traditional gospel away from its insistence on repentance and faith in God's substitutionary atoning sacrifice in exchange for God's *imprimatur* of righteousness. Instead, Wright would have us believe that all who dedicate themselves to Christ and follow-through with behaviors consistent with His ethics are in God's family and belong at His table. The late philosopher and author Dallas Willard (another favorite among revisionist evangelicals) would seem to concur when he remarks, "It isn't that we become righteous by having the correct beliefs. We become righteous by trusting God and living from Him."[19] In the same interview, Willard declares it is a mistake to think that "God has a list of things you must believe, and then He'll have to let you into heaven."[20]

Jesus: Heaven's Dress Code Enforcer

So which are we to believe? Is the gospel the imputation of Christ's righteousness in the form of a holy robe to all who repent and (in Willard's sardonic lexicon) "believe the right things," or is it Wright's version of covenant membership that comes to all would-be disciples of Christ as they live out their faith in obedience to His teaching? Does the Bible provide any insight on this critical divide?

Indeed it does, and from no less an expert than Jesus Christ Himself. In **Matthew 22:1-14,** Jesus tells a parable to

---

[18] Phil Johnson, "What's Wrong with Wright?" Ligonier Ministries, https://www.ligonier.org/learn/articles/whats-wrong-wright-examining-new-perspective-paul/

[19] Dallas Willard, interview with John Ortberg, Menlo Park Presbyterian Church, Menlo Park, CA, Dec. 13, 2009.

[20] Dallas Willard, interview with John Ortberg.

His disciples, the ending of which addresses this exact issue. At a banquet meant to represent the eternal celebration between God and His true companions, Jesus tells of someone God deems unacceptable at the feast—an unwelcome intruder. In an astonishing turn of events, this impostor is confronted by the King, the Lord Jesus Christ, and summarily tossed from the banquet into outer darkness, a figurative description for hell.

For what crime? The King Himself had declared that invitations were to be sent far and wide, to whomever could be found (**v. 9**). Not only that, invitations were sent out without regard to one's moral standing (**v. 10**); in fact, the event was to include (**v. 10**) "**both bad and good**." The man is at the banquet when confronted by the Lord, implying his intention to participate in the communal gathering. Ostensibly he is there on the basis of fulfilling his part in a "covenant of vocation" while on Earth. There is no mention of any obvious treachery, and his presence at the banquet would presume at least an outward demonstration of allegiance to the King. None of his fellow celebrants seem to have any inclination that the man's admission to the event was illegitimate.

So why did Christ throw him out of the celebration and into hell? *For one reason alone.* In the midst of the celebration, Christ discovers the man and asks him a single question: "**'Friend, how did you get in here without a wedding garment?' And he was speechless. Then the king said to the attendants, 'Bind him hand and foot and cast him into the outer darkness. In that place there will be weeping and gnashing of teeth'**" (**Luke 22:12-13**).

This is most extraordinary. Jesus confronts a would-be disciple and fellow celebrant at His kingdom celebration and forth-with tosses him into hell for violating the dress code! Jesus is saying that whether or not you are wearing the proper wedding garb in His presence will determine whether you celebrate with Him forever, or whether He orders you cast into hell. Jesus' words leave no doubt as to His implication: no matter what, it is *vital* to be found wearing the proper wedding garment in the presence of God!

So let's take Christ's teaching and apply it to what we have already learned. From the Scriptures referenced above, we can deduce:

> (1) The wedding dress Christ requires comes entirely through the initiative and activity of God (**Isa 61:10**);

> (2) The process includes the removal of the soiled garment of the sinner in exchange for God's righteous robe (**Zech 3:4**); and,

> (3) The event must occur *prior to* one's meeting with the Lord Himself (**Matt 22:11-13**).

Compare this with Wright. On all three measures, Wright's theology misses the mark. How so?

> (1) Wright's ideas would introduce a disciple's faithful obedience as a factor in determining his acceptance before God, in violation of **Isaiah 61:10**.

> (2) Wright's theology minimizes or negates altogether the gospel's insistence on a specific garment exchange which represents a cleansing of

the sinner's stained nature, in violation of **Zechariah 3:4**. And finally,

(3) Wright insists that no one will be justified, or declared righteous—*including, by analogy, wearing any robe of righteousness*—until he reaches Heaven. This perspective dismisses outright any prerequisite dress code that must be applied prior to the afterlife and one's ultimate encounter with Lord Jesus Christ, in clear violation of the Lord's own teaching in **Matthew 22:11-13.**

On all three accounts, Wright's ideas oppose the distinct and indisputable instruction of the Word of God.

Conclusion: What Are *You* Wearing?

Make no mistake. Whether they recognize it or not, those who tamper with the Bible's wondrous and clear presentation of God's provision of a holy garment to penitent believers, made through faith in Christ's penal substitutionary atonement, do so from the corruption and pride of their carnal selves. It arises from the age-old, grotesque desire to offer up some form of human activity designed to merit God's acceptance. These would-be spiritual leaders and religious teachers resent God's impossible righteous standard, so they devise one of their own. Here, **Proverbs 14:9** applies: **"Fools mock at the guilt offering, but the upright enjoy acceptance."** Those who dislike God's bar of approval will mock at what He has done to reconcile repentant and believing sinners to Himself. But rather than enjoying God's acceptance, they are counted as fools.

Why do such fools mock in this way? Most commonly, it is because they do not want to share in the persecution Christ says will come to His true followers (**Gal 6:12**; see also **John 15:18-25; 16:1-4; 2 Tim 3:12; 1 John 3:13**). Those who deny the doctrine of substitutionary atonement do so to avoid telling sinners they have neither the autonomous will nor ability to merit any favor of God (**Phil 2:12**), that they live under God's contemporary judgment even now (**John 3:18, 36; Gal 3:10**), and that apart from faith in Christ's Person and saving work, they are headed for eternal punishment (**Matt 25:46; John 8:24**). That is exclusive, divisive, even inflammatory language, and those who deny the true gospel message want no part in such polemical discourse that might invite rejection and open hostility.[21]

However, such a polemic is *precisely* the intent of the true gospel, which is why Christ is depicted in both the Old and New Testaments as a "**rock of offense**" (**Isa 8:14; Rom 9:33; 1 Pet 2:8**). The gospel is a polemical message designed to convict the sinner of damning sin and the utter ineptitude of any self-rescue. It is, therefore, by its very nature *offensive*. Because humans are hard-wired to believe their estimable efforts can improve their standing before God, these modern-day evangelical revisionists have a ready-made market of like-minded sycophants. All they need to do to maintain their popular standing is appeal to human pride. But none of this is new. These latest attempts to undermine God's righteous standard are but recycled heresies which, regardless of the age or form, are subject to the same chilling and dire sentence Christ gave to the improperly-clothed wedding celebrant.

N.T. Wright, Dallas Willard and all who follow in the wake of their teaching on justification are mistaken. Heaven

---

[21] For further discussion of the persecution the Bible promises will come to all faithful believers, see chapter 8.

has a dress code, and it is strictly enforced. The robe of righteousness that must be worn in the presence of Christ has no input from human hands, comes through the imputation of Christ's righteousness in exchange for the penitent believer's sins, and must be applied by Christ alone prior to the one's progression to the afterlife. This is the clear statement of Scripture. May God continue to call forth an army of righteously robed converts to proclaim His true gospel, and to rebuke all assaults against it.

7

Beware False Camaraderie
Opposing Syncretistic Efforts

The primary predisposing factor to spiritual naiveté is biblical illiteracy. When professing believers are ignorant of what God's Word actually says, they open themselves to a whole host of erroneous ideas. One particular menace is *syncretism*, which is the melding of the true with the false. Throughout history, Satan has found the ground of biblical illiteracy fertile soil for his syncretistic efforts to merge all sorts of his heresies into what is held to be true. One sinister heresy in our times enjoying particular success within modern evangelicalism is the false notion of evolution. Its penetration into today's evangelical church comes via a variety of quasi-Christian formats, where appeals are made to "broad-minded evangelicals" to lay down arms and come to some general agreement as to what the Bible says about origins. "After all," these appeals will argue, "we believe in Jesus as Savior and Lord and in the authority of Scripture essentially as you do."[22]

---

[22] One such platform is Biologos (www.biologos.org), whose subheading reads "God's Word, God's world."

These appeals, mind you, always seem to arise from those proposing an alternative to the straightforward reading of the text, one which will update our biblical understanding based upon "new revelations" from the worlds of both "science" and "biblical scholarship." We are now being told by "experts" how "ancient Near East cultural understanding" can broaden our grasp of how the Bible reconciles with the world we see around us. The articles always seem to be written as if truly enlightened evangelicals have no problem with the latest learning and have advanced well beyond these core proposals, but here are some basics that even evangelical Neanderthals (pardon the pun) should be able to get behind.

One such appeal comes from Todd Wilson, president and co-founder of the *Center for Pastor Theologians*.[23] Wilson begins by disclosing how, some time ago, his conservative-on-many-issues congregation had some "heartburn" when its closely held, literal six-day creation scheme was assaulted by its new pastor's belief in evolutionary creationism. This understandably led to a "tension-filled season," during which the church "grappled" with its "doctrinal boundaries." The upshot of this grappling was the codification of "ten theses on creation and evolution that we believe (most) evangelicals can (mostly) affirm," what they termed (in an apparent nod to C.S. Lewis) "Mere Creation."

How did this endeavor play out, as one among the many you will encounter if you train your spiritual eyes for their presence? The following is a commentary on their evolutionary "Wittenberg door:"

---

[23] Todd Wilson, "Ten Theses on Creation and Evolution That (Most) Evangelicals Can Support," in *Christianity Today*, Jan. 4, 2019. https://www.christianitytoday.com/ct/2019/january-web-only/ten-theses-creation-evolution-evangelicals.html. All quotes of Wilson throughout this chapter are referenced from this article.

1. The doctrine of creation is central to the Christian faith.

They got this one right, though probably not in the manner they intended. In fact, this is a dead-on, stand-alone truth. Wilson proposes that the doctrine of creation belongs in the same strata as the doctrines of the Father, Christ, the Spirit, and soteriology at the core of the Christian faith, and he is absolutely correct. Make no mistake: Genesis 1-2 is so vital to proper biblical understanding that if one does not comprehend it rightly, one will err repeatedly in attempting to assimilate the remainder of the Word of God. Want to know a simple way to confirm one has found a biblical church that likely gets the gospel right and upholds sound doctrine in other areas? Ask its pastor if he reads and teaches Genesis 1-2 in a literal, grammatical, historical manner. The correlation is astounding.

2. The Bible, both Old and New Testaments, is the Word of God, inspired, authoritative, and without error. Therefore whatever Scripture teaches is to be believed as God's instruction, without denying that the human authors of Scripture communicated using the cultural conventions of their time.

Here, again, they got it right—mostly. We might add to the inspiration, authority and inerrancy of the Word of God its completeness, sufficiency, perspicuity, necessity, efficacy, certainty, immutability, universality, vitality, and theo-centricity, as these qualities are no less applicable to the Word of God. But we concede the point. Further, it is axiomatic that whatever Scripture teaches is to be believed as God's instruction. In other words, when the Bible speaks, God speaks.

The dog whistle in Thesis #2 comes in the last clause. Wilson writes, "No amount of stress on a 'high view of the Bible' should cause us to inadvertently downplay the human side of the equation."[24] Okay, fair enough on its face. The Bible did have human authors who wrote according to "cultural conventions" of their time. If that is all that is intended, fine. And if he is also implying that readers of the Bible must be attuned to the grammatical and contextual aspects of the writing, more power to him.

But if the implication is that the humanity of the Bible's authors somehow obscures God's actual message and thereby diminishes our confidence in understanding it, he is incorrect. The humanity of the authors of Scripture does not in any way confound the communication of God in His Word. Just because the Bible had human authors beginning 3500 years ago does not mean that their "cultural conventions" somehow limit our modern comprehension of what they were saying and how it applies today. God inspired His human authors and their "cultural conventions" to say exactly what He meant to say and how He meant to say it, with a message that transcends time, as comprehendible today as it was to those to whom it was first written.

3. Genesis 1-2 is historical in nature, rich in literary artistry, and theological in purpose. These chapters should be read with the intent of discerning what God says through what the human author has said.

Wilson begins to reveal his true colors in his commentary on Thesis #3 when he writes, "Of course, there is much to debate about how to interpret Genesis 1-2" (those colors come into even greater relief later in the article when he

---

24 Wilson, "Ten Theses."

favorably references theologian Karl Barth and historian Mark Noll, as well as his use of the NRSV). He goes on to suggest the need for "a balanced approach to the question of the literary genre of Genesis 1-2." Wilson subdivides Genesis 1-2 into a proposed composite of historical, theological and literary types, and insinuates that if this portion of Scripture can be designated as literary and theological as well as history, it would somehow diminish its reliability as a source of historical information.

Says who? Only those trying to retain some claim to orthodoxy as they simultaneously seek to undermine the information of the text by reclassifying it as something other than history. So let us be clear here: Genesis 1-2 is *history*. A sixth-grade student can identify it as such. Yes, the text does yield tremendous theological implications, as any biblical historical text might, and it has a certain literary style. But neither of those designations alters in any way the factual, historical information we are reading about the world and its occupants. Genesis 1-2 is God's clear-cut revelation of how things began, designed to inform the highest order of His creation about something they would have no other way of knowing. Only those who wish to impose faulty paradigms on Scripture have any inclination to consider Genesis 1-2 as some form of literature other than history (e.g. legend or poetry), as if that literary designation might somehow disable its plainly evident interpretation.

4. God created and sustains everything. This means that he is as much involved in natural processes as he is in supernatural events. Creation itself provides unmistakable evidence of God's handiwork.

Again, pretty good, up to a point. God certainly has created everything and sustains it moment by moment (**Job 12:10;**

Acts 17:28; Heb 1:3). His direct handiwork is no less a part of natural processes as it is with supernatural ones. Wilson makes a good point about the tendency even of evangelical Christians toward *deistic* thinking, often slipping "into patterns of thinking that exclude God from the routine workings of nature, like the rotation of the stars, the formation of clouds, or the grass as it grows." He rightly references Psalm 104 as evidence of God's continuous, direct ordering of the natural world.

But the Bible nowhere states nor implies that study of the natural world can divulge any knowledge about its origins. Yes, as Wilson offers, **"the heavens declare the glory of God"** (**Ps 19:1**), but not in any way that brings to light the process that led to their formation. In fact, it is no coincidence that after David extols the natural, or *general,* revelation of the cosmos in the first portion of this Psalm (**Ps 19:1-6**), he follows it with an exquisite overview of the *special* revelation encompassed in the Word of God (**Ps 19:7-11**). Why this juxtaposition of the general and special revelation of God? David knows that general revelation only goes so far in revealing who God is and what He has done. David knows that ultimate knowledge of God and His work must come from His self-revelation as can only be found in His Word (i.e. *special revelation* as opposed to *natural revelation*).

5. Adam and Eve were real persons in a real past, and the fall was a real event with real and devastating consequences for the entire human race.

Wilson gets this thesis exactly right as stated, which is commendable. But his substantiating commentary is so problematic that it leads him to decidedly unbiblical conclusions. Yes, Adam and Eve were real persons in the real past, who really fell with real and devastating consequences for each and every one of their descendants. Wilson then (correctly) reports that this reality is under considerable challenge within modern evangelical Christianity. Why is that? Because, according to Wilson, "the genetic evidence, at least as we now understand it, makes belief in an original human pair doubtful if not impossible." He then predicts, ". . . in 20 years' time, support for Adam and Eve as real persons in a real past will be a minority view even within evangelicalism." And what if that happens? Wilson continues: "Should this come to pass, I remain confident that the Christian faith will survive, even though this will require some reconfiguration of our deepest convictions."

Just how "Christian faith will survive" despite the "reconfiguration" of its "deepest convictions" is not at all clear from Wilson. In reality, this would be an utter impossibility, because when a faith reconfigures its deepest convictions, then that faith is no longer said to exist. Give up a real Adam and Eve with a real fall bringing real consequences to the entire human race, and you might as well describe a new religion, for you have just severed orthodox Christianity from its doctrinal moorings. To deny a real Adam and Eve is to call the Bible erroneous and God a liar, because He says all humans derive from this original pair (**Gen 3:20; Acts 17:26**). To deny a real Adam and Eve is to contradict the Lord and Savior, Jesus Christ, who references them as the basis for understanding God's concept of marriage (cf. **Matt 19:4; Mark 10:6**). And to deny a real Adam is to nullify the manner by which God says humans might be reconciled to Him, because the only ones He justifies are those born into sin through Adam and then reborn into righteousness through Christ (**John 3:3-7; Rom 5:15-19; 1 Cor 15:45-49**).

Wilson says Paul's argument in Romans 5 along with Adam's presence in genealogies (**Gen 5; Luke 1**) keeps him tethered—for now—to the traditional view of a real Adam and Eve, but he leaves open the possibility that future scientific developments might cause him to reconsider. Which begs the question: what might those future "scientific developments" be? Science relies upon the *certain* operation of uniform constants. Given that, on what basis can we be certain that the scientific constants we can measure today, such as the speed of light, were operating in the same manner at the moment of creation? We cannot. So if we are only *speculating* that the constants of today were present in unchanged form at creation, how then are conclusions based upon such speculation "scientific?" This is an unsolved quandary for Wilson and his entire evolutionary ilk.

The same goes for the "genetic evidence" to which Wilson alludes. Wilson is basing his conclusions upon genetic similarities found between humans and certain other species. But genetic similarity does not confirm shared ancestry. Moreover, genetic makeup today depends not only upon genetic makeup at the moment of creation—which, again, cannot at all be known or proven—but also upon modern theories of inheritance patterns remaining stable since the moment God initiated His creation plan. This is not a given by any stretch, meaning the uniformity upon which scientific study relies cannot be relied upon here. In fact, given how the Bible presents pre-Fall/post-Fall and pre-flood/post-flood physical realities as substantially different (average human lifespans being just one example), hypothesizing no impact of these events upon genetic assumptions represents a very giant and *non-scientific* leap of faith—whether one admits to it or not.

On a textual level, whatever happened to Wilson's "full-throated" endorsement of inerrancy he proclaims at the beginning of his article? As an inerrantist leader of "pastor theologians," one presumes Wilson would always subject his doctrinal beliefs to the exact text of Scripture. Specifically, we expect him to know that when God uses the term *bara* for "created" in the first statement in His Word, He is specifying that such a work is ineligible for scientific inquiry. As opposed to the other Hebrew terms for "create" in the Old Testament (e.g. *yatsar* and *asah*), the term *bara* is used only with God as its subject, and only in the creation of marvels never before known. The use of the term denotes a development of something completely outside the boundary of the established order, and not subject to the constraints of uniformity that govern science. As such, God's use of the verb *bara* in the first verse of His first book should notify all to pay attention, because the information that follows cannot be discerned through observation of natural phenomena (i.e. scientific inquiry). In fact, this is exactly why **Hebrews 11:3** says it is **"by faith"** (and by implication, not "by sight," meaning scientific inquiry) **we understand that the universe was created by the Word of God, so that what is seen was not made out of things that are visible."** In other words, do you want to know about the world at the time of creation? Then look to the Word of God, in faith, and to that Word only.

Untroubled by this, Wilson then proceeds to a very troubling deduction: "It may be the case that faithful Christians will develop biblically legitimate and theologically sensible ways of explaining the gospel apart from a real Adam and Eve." For someone claiming to uphold the inerrancy of Scripture, this is certainly an incongruous detour. How in the world could Christians ever be "faithful" by refuting what God has explicitly said about this pair of original humans? And how would a revised "gospel" look if the "last Adam" did not become a "life-giving spirit" because the "first Adam" never became a "living being?" (**1 Cor 15:45**)? Apart from a real Adam and Eve, the entire structure of Christianity as presented in God's Word becomes a house of cards.

Finally, instead of a clarion call to defend God's Word against any and all specious theories masquerading as knowledge, Wilson concludes, " . . . the better part of wisdom is maintaining a spirit of *engaged conversation* on this issue" (italics his). Really? What happened to the New Testament's repeated calls for the vigorous censure of falsehood (**2 Tim 4:2; Titus 1:9; Eph 5:11; 2 Cor 10:5; 2 John 8-11; Jude 3-4**)? It is the harbinger of apostasy for professing believers to have their doctrinal convictions always subject to supposed discoveries of worldly knowledge, be they scientific or sociologic. Paul warns the Colossians they should, "**See to it that no one takes you captive through philosophy and empty deception, according to the tradition of men, according to the elementary principles of the world, rather than according to Christ**" (**Col 2:8**)—the precise muddle in which Wilson, by his own words, appears to find himself.

6. Human beings are created in the image of God and are thus unique among God's creatures. They possess special dignity within creation.

This is a true statement, taken right out of **Genesis 1:26-28**. But don't miss how Wilson's embrace of evolutionary creationism places himself in a real pickle as a result of this thesis. Evolutionary creationists cannot say that the version of humans we see today are the ones made in God's image.

Why not? Because evolution presumes the human species, like every species, is constantly progressing to a more highly developed form through environmental adaptation. In an evolutionary paradigm, every species is always evolving to a higher order of being, *and this must also include humans*. Thus, for the evolutionary creationist, there is no way around this dilemma: either humans are never quite made in God's image, because they continue to evolve, or they are made in God's image because God is evolving just as they are. Both are profoundly unbiblical perspectives.

7. There is no final conflict between the Bible rightly understood and the facts of science rightly understood. God's "two books," Scripture and nature, ultimately agree. Therefore Christians should approach the claims of contemporary science with both interest and discernment, confident that all truth is God's truth.

Two books of infallible truth? Hardly. Jesus declares God's Word to be truth (**John 17:17**). He says, ". . . **If you abide in my Word . . . you will know the truth.....**" (John 8:31-32). Thus, believers can be certain that if their convictions about anything—natural or spiritual—are anchored to the Word of God, they will always be aligned with God's truth. But God never made the same promise about His creation. He never said to anchor oneself according to discoveries about the natural world made by finite minds. He never said that the origin of the universe and everything in it could be uncovered using scientific constants of today applied to the beginning of time. *In fact, He says the exact opposite.*

In Chapter 3 of his second epistle, Peter specifically instructs the reader not to assume uniformity of natural processes at the beginning and end of time. He writes that foolish scoffers will be the ones to say, ". . . **all things are**

continuing as they were from the beginning of creation"
(**v. 4**), with the obvious implication that you do not want to
be a foolish scoffer. Peter goes on to reveal catastrophic
events outside the bounds of uniformity marked the creation
of this world, and will also mark its end. Using this paradigm,
where uniformity of nature is not presumed at the bookends
of time, we have a framework from which to acknowledge
the uniformity we see in the present, while at the same time
we can trust the Bible's literal rendering of how the world
began and how it will end.

Note also that if you take Wilson's "two books" proposal
to its logical conclusion, it actually makes all truth relative.
How so? Wilson contends his two sources of truth will
ultimately agree, but he admits that this might only be seen in
eternity. Until then, what happens when they yield conflicting
conclusions? Which source gets the final say? The Bible?
Science? Sometimes one and sometimes the other, whichever
seems to be the most compelling? That is the definition of
relativism, and is certainly not the approach of a biblical
inerrantist. Ironically, this *was* the approach of the mainline
Protestant church and other institutions (e.g. Fuller Seminary)
in the 20th century, when in a Faustian bargain they
surrendered biblical inerrancy in order to curry favor with the
world. The result? A landscape of institutions fast declining
into irrelevancy, having no discernible sign of (nor any
interest in) biblical orthodoxy whatsoever. Mark this:
whenever one sees the proposed "two books" paradigm in
operation, the Bible is *always* subordinated to the latest so-
called "scientific" discovery, with a predictable corresponding
deterioration into heterodoxy, then apostasy, and ultimately
heresy.

8. The Christian faith is compatible with different scientific theories of origins, from young-earth creationism to evolutionary creationism, but it is incompatible with any view that rejects God as the Creator and Sustainer of all things. Christians can (and do) differ on their assessment of the merits of various scientific theories of origins.

The Christian faith is *not* compatible with evolutionary creationism, theistic evolution, or whatever term of the day is in vogue. But don't take my word for it. This assessment is according to the ultimate Master, the Lord Jesus Christ Himself. Where? As noted previously, Jesus Himself refers to the creation of Adam and Eve as a historical event in **Mark 10:6 (Matt 19:4;** cf. **Exod 20:11)**, where He quotes from both **Gen 1:27** and **5:2: "But from the beginning of creation, 'God made them male and female.'"** In those twelve words, Jesus utterly refutes the underpinnings of evolutionary theory.

How so? First, Jesus uses the past tense—"made"—to confirm the creation of the first humans as a finished product. In other words, the process was immediate and complete, not developmental and ongoing, as must be the case with evolution. Second, Jesus states that this male and female were created **"from the beginning of creation,"** and not billions of years after the world was formed. And since— according to Jesus—humans were created **"from the beginning of creation,"** the sixth day on which they were created must have so close in time to the first as to be nearly indistinguishable in the whole of creation. Third, by claiming that, **"from the beginning, God made them male and female,"** Jesus is here establishing human sexual reproduction as the means by which the species has procreated from its inception. This statement of Jesus invalidates the possibility that humans could have ever derived from single cell organisms via asexual reproduction. With an eloquence and economy of words that only the Lord Himself could devise, Jesus completely exposes and repudiates the lie of evolution.

How do we know Jesus was referring to a specific Adam and Eve in His reference to male and female originating at the beginning of creation? From the context of Jesus' statement. In Mark 10, Jesus is explaining God's perspective on marriage and divorce. As He continues (**Mark 10:7-8**), Jesus quotes **Genesis 2:24**: **"'For this reason a man shall leave his father and mother and be joined to his wife, and the two shall become one flesh.'"** To what reason is Jesus referring? He is referencing the prior verse in **Genesis 2:23**: **"'Then the man said, 'This at last is bone of my bones and flesh of my flesh; she shall be called Woman, because she was taken out of Man.'"** What man? The *only* man referenced in Genesis 2, and actually named in verse 20: *Adam*. Thus, these verses specifically relate to the instantaneous and mature creation of woman from Adam. In fact, the only man and the only woman in the Bible up until this point were the first man and woman, Adam and Eve. So, by referencing Genesis 2, Jesus unambiguously affirms His belief in the creation of a literal Adam and Eve on the sixth day of the earth's existence. It may be that, according to Wilson, "Christians can (and do) differ on their assessment of the merits of various scientific theories of origins." But Jesus is clear where He stands on the issue.

9. Christians should be well grounded in the Bible's teaching on creation but always hold their views with humility, respecting the convictions of others and not aggressively advocating for positions on which evangelicals disagree.

This thesis is in itself an oxymoron. Ask yourself, how can Christians be "well-grounded" in the Bible's teaching on creation," and yet not defend that ground when confronted with any challenge to that ground? Being "well-grounded," by definition, *means to stand your ground*. It means to understand something in a way that will not move you from your foundation. Well-grounded Ph.D. students are expected to make a defense of their foundation of knowledge when their course of study is complete; no degree ensues without it! But Wilson wants well-grounded students of creation to bend at the slightest breeze of opposition, if that opposition is coming from someone who professes to be of the same faith. This isn't biblical humility; this is post-modern, theological drivel. Following this advice, Jesus would have remained politely silent or even agreeable when Satan presented Him with what *he* had learned from Scripture (**Matt 4:6**). As it happened, Jesus did not respect the conviction of another (in this case, the devil), but rather aggressively advocated an opposing position, rebuking Satan's false interpretation of Scripture with His own true interpretation (**Matt 4:7**).

In contrast to Wilson's idea, biblical humility occurs when one completely submits one's own contemplations of the world to God and His Word. The humblest Christians are those who stay most true to the Word of God, not letting the appearances of the world disengage them from commitment to the truth of the text (**Prov 3:5-6**). This goes against the trend in post-modern evangelical Christianity, where a so-called "hermeneutic of humility" has arisen, which in reality is nothing of the sort. This hermeneutic suggests that certainty and intransigence in presenting one's own convictions on a topic of controversy is arrogant and spiritually immature. Wilson claims, "In practice, humility and a desire to preserve ecclesial unity mean respectfully listening to the views of others. It also means not agitating for change or grandstanding with one's own views. On a complex, sensitive, and contentious issue like origins, it is best for evangelicals of goodwill not to aggressively advocate for positions on which evangelicals disagree." Elsewhere he writes, "It is a sign of childhood or adolescence to be agitated by a less than black-and-white world."

Really? Jesus was polemically agitated in His hostile interaction with the Pharisees on "complex, sensitive and contentious issues," such as the kingdom of God, proselytizing, the Sabbath, tithing, persecution of His faithful messengers and the like (**Matt 23:1-36**). Later in the New Testament, the Apostle Paul writes that we are to be imitators of him, as he is of Christ (**1 Cor 11:1**). So what does Paul recommend when the truth of God's Word is under assault, passive regard or confident rebuke? His model is Christ as he compels the church in Corinth to, " . . . **destroy arguments and every lofty opinion raised against the knowledge of God, and take every thought captive to obey Christ, being ready to punish every disobedience, when your obedience is complete**" (**2 Cor 10:5-6**). So Jesus gets agitated when the black-and-white instruction of God is assailed, and Paul does the same. How can the true believer do anything less?

Why was Paul so indignant at arguments and lofty opinions raised against what God has said in His Word?

Because false teaching in one area has a way of spreading to all areas, and with false teaching comes proclivity to sin; the book of Jude lays this out plainly. Because of this, Paul writes to that same church in Corinth, **"Who is made to fall** (i.e. drawn into sin)**, and I am not indignant?"** (**2 Cor 11:29b**). According to Paul, righteous indignation in the face of false teaching is the appropriate and indeed, *biblically prescribed* reaction for those who would establish themselves as true followers of Christ. It has been said that one sign of Christian maturity is when God is dishonored and you feel the insult. Now obviously, not every theological difference is a polemical hill on which to die. But as we have already established with Thesis #1, the issues at stake if a literal, historical view of Genesis 1-2 is surrendered are comprehensively devastating to the Christian faith. This is why, on the issue of creationism versus evolution, the admonition of Paul pertains:

> . . . the Lord's servant must not be quarrelsome but kind to everyone, able to teach, patiently enduring evil, correcting his opponents with gentleness. God may perhaps grant them repentance leading to a knowledge of the truth, and they may come to their senses and escape from the snare of the devil, after being captured by him to do his will (2 Tim 2:24-26).

10. Everything in creation finds its source, goal, and meaning in Jesus Christ, in whom the whole of creation will one day achieve eschatological redemption and renewal. All things will be united in him, things in heaven and things on earth.

This is the sort of statement one expects from someone who is not a true biblical inerrantist, and therefore struggles to comprehend the true plan of God, as found in His Word. It is true that Jesus Christ is the source of creation (**John 1:3; Col 1:16; Heb 1:3**), that all things presently hold together in Him (**Col 1:17**), and that, in time, all things will be united in Him (**Eph 1:10**). It is not true that everything in creation finds its source in Jesus Christ, for that would make Him the Author of evil, which the Bible repudiates (**Hab 1:13; James 1:13; 1 John 1:5**). It is also untrue that the "whole of creation will one day achieve eschatological redemption and renewal." Much of creation is headed for devastation and ruin, when Jesus returns to judge the earth, inflicting vengeance and promising eternal destruction on those who rebel against God and do not obey the gospel of the Lord Jesus (**2 Thess 1:8-9**). We'll concede Wilson's larger point is true, that ultimately everything in this world—*including evil*—is ordained for the glory that the Father is bestowing upon His Son. But the Son's preeminence above all things is precisely why it is so important to see what Christ has to say about origins (see Thesis #8 above). Since our Master's position on origins negates any consideration of evolution, so must our own.

As you can see, the theses upon which Wilson and his church have joined in agreement on the issue of creationism versus evolution leave much to be desired. These ten "theses" should cause the biblically committed believer to grieve for both Wilson and his congregation; Wilson for his meager understanding of both biblical inerrancy and the limits of science, and his congregation for their error in judgment that brought him to their pulpit. No effort to bridge the divide between those who believe in some sort of evolutionary creationism and those who hold fast to a literal creation scheme will ever be successful. While one side holds fast to the truth of the text, the other routinely jettisons these textual convictions whenever human reasoning based upon so-called "science" commands, regardless of formal claims to inerrancy or a "high view" of Scripture. And once one begins to allegorize the Scripture to accord with the unsubstantiated conjectures of finite minds, where is the end point? Why stop playing fast and loose with Scripture at Genesis 2? In fact, most evolutionary creationists do not stop there, which is why most who side with evolution also stray into ideas of egalitarianism, supersecessionism, preterism, post-millennialism, and similar sorts of theological error. Wilson's article should stimulate biblically faithful believers to commit themselves to uphold the biblical record of Genesis 1-2 in a literal historical manner, and refute those who would peddle any evolutionary alternative.

8

Beware False Predictions

Debunking the "Irresistibility" of Christian Faith and Its "Likeable" Adherents

"How do I know if I am a true Christian?"

Have you ever asked yourself that question? God says you should. Paul writes to the Corinthian church, **"Examine yourselves, to see whether you are in the faith. Test yourselves. Or do you not realize this about yourselves, that Jesus Christ is in you?—unless indeed you fail to meet the test!"** (2 Cor 13:5). So those who desire to be true followers of Jesus Christ are expected to assess whether Jesus truly lives within. How is this done?

This question was anticipated and answered by the Lord Jesus Himself. He told a group of recent Jewish believers, **"If you abide in my Word, you are truly My disciples, and you will know the truth, and the truth will set you free"** (John 8:31b-32). So according to Jesus, the criterion for knowing who truly belongs to Him is fidelity to His Word, which brings knowledge of truth, which brings everlasting freedom from sin—its penalty, its power and (one day) its presence altogether.

Well, how hard could that be—staying true to Jesus' Word? One look at the modern evangelical church would indicate *harder than you might think*. In fact, one of the most appalling realities of our present day is how many would-be faithful followers of Christ regularly imbibe teaching that is not only not what Christ taught, *but is in fact the exact opposite!* And of all the topics where what the Bible teaches and what is commonly taught as true are most at odds, at or near the top is the anticipated response of the world to the Christ-led life.

Take, for example, a recent book from the pastor of one of America's largest churches. In it, he claims that if Christ-followers were to live out the faith as was originally taught and exampled by Christ, the appeal of that faith would be *irresistible* to a watching world. Similarly, another American megachurch pastor and popular author not long ago exposited **Matthew 5:20** for his congregation as follows:

> To understand Jesus, we might actually translate Matthew 5, verse 20—a really core statement in the Sermon on the Mount—'Unless your 'likeability' surpasses that of the Pharisees and the teachers of the law, you cannot enter the kingdom of heaven.' We think of righteousness as this kind of cliché, pious thing, but really it's very much . . . to be a likable, caring, loving person.

Is that true? Is the authentically lived, Christ-led life "irresistible" to a watching world? And is "likeability" an anticipated assessment we should expect those outside the

Church to attach to the genuine Christ follower? What is the biblical testimony in this regard?

Answer: it would be hard to parody what the Bible has to say more outrageously. The modern evangelical notion that authentic Christianity and its eminently "likeable" Christ-followers should be "irresistible" to the surrounding world could not be further from what the Bible actually says. This would even qualify as outrageous lampoon—such as from The Babylon Bee—were it not for the fact that these teachers are one hundred percent serious. As it is, the only way such evangelical charlatans can get away with this scandalous deception is that their listeners must never bother to open and read the Bible.

Here is how "irresistible" Christianity was at its outset. Nearly two years into Christ's ministry, the question on the mind of one witness was: **"Lord, will those who are saved be few?"** **(Luke 13:23)**. And Jesus does not contradict this assessment, but informs His followers that the path to salvation is *agonizing!* (Agonizing paths, it should be obvious, are *not* irresistible.) Then, by the end of Christ's earthly tenure, after thousands upon thousands had heard His message while eating divinely-prepared food and being miraculously healed of every condition imaginable, the sum total of believers was not many more than 120 in an upper room in Jerusalem (**Acts 1:15**), and 500 up in Galilee (**1 Cor 15:6**). Even given generous approximations, the "conversion rate" to Christianity while the Son of God walked the earth seems to have been in the neighborhood of 0.1%—hardly an "irresistible" number.

As for the "likeability" of true believers, Jesus says to those He sent out during His ministry, **"You will be hated by all for my name's sake"** (**Matt 10:22**) (Likeability, it should be obvious, does *not* induce hatred.) He says of the future destiny of His followers in His Olivet Discourse, **"Then they will deliver you up to tribulation and put you to death, and you will be hated by all nations for My name's sake"** (**Matt 24:9**). And in **John 15:19**, He declares to His Apostles, **"If you were of the world, the world would love you as its own; but because you are not of the world, therefore the world hates you."** So, according to Jesus, the faithful life of believers engenders hatred from the world, a far cry from "likeability."

Well, maybe these were ominous predictions of Christ simply because He knew that His fallible followers would fall so far short of His example. But Christ was "likeable" while here in earthly form, wasn't He? After all, if we as Christians are to be His "likeable" followers, our Mentor must have epitomized this quality, right? The answer is found in **John 7:7**, where Jesus says to His brothers (who, at this point, were not yet believers in Him), **"The world cannot hate you, but it hates Me because I testify about it that its works are evil."** And in **John 15:18** and **20**, Jesus provides clarification to His above warning (cf. **John 15:19**) to His Apostles: **"If the world hates you, know that it hated Me before it hated you . . . Remember the word that I said to you: 'A servant is not greater than his Master.' If they persecuted Me, they will persecute you."**

Wow. Jesus says He wasn't likeable because of His message, and His Apostles were given the same unpopular message, guaranteed to make them pariahs. So Jesus was hated, as were His Apostles. But maybe that all changes by the time the Church gets off the ground. Doesn't God want His church to be popular? Isn't that how it grows, through pragmatic, "seeker-friendly" methods designed to optimize the appeal of Jesus? What is the expectation of the New Testament writers on this topic?

To this, we find that Peter's expectation of revulsion and mistreatment for faithfulness to Christ is no different from Jesus' day. He informs his readers:

> **Beloved, do not be surprised at the fiery trial when it comes upon you to test you, as though something strange were happening to you. But rejoice insofar as you share Christ's sufferings, that you may also rejoice and be glad when His glory is revealed. If you are insulted for the name of Christ, you are blessed, because the Spirit of glory and of God rests upon you (1 Pet 4:12-14).**

Paul, too, anticipates the unpopular nature of Christianity and its converts when he preaches in Lystra that entrance to the kingdom of God is fraught with many tribulations (**Acts 14:22**). In **2 Corinthians 11:23-28**, Paul itemizes exactly how "resistible" his message was as he details the litany of imprisonments, beatings, and near-death experiences that it brought. And toward the end of his ministry, he writes to Timothy, "**Indeed, all who desire to live a godly life in Christ Jesus will be persecuted**" (**2 Tim 3:12**).

So, the anticipation of Jesus and His Apostles is animosity and persecution for the faithful, just as Christ Himself received. They anticipate that most will reject the far-from-irresistible message of repentance for the forgiveness of sins (cf. **Luke 24:47**), and will turn on those who devotedly proclaim this gospel. In fact, the atrocious interpretation of "righteousness" as "likeability" in **Matthew 5:20** is especially egregious, because not only did Jesus teach the exact

109

opposite, but He did so only moments earlier in the same talk! Jesus says:

> **Blessed are those who are persecuted for righteousness sake, for theirs is the kingdom of heaven. Blessed are you when others revile you and persecute you and utter all kinds of evil against you falsely on My account. Rejoice and be glad, for your reward is great in heaven, for so they persecuted the prophets who were before you (Matt 5:10-12).**

Clearly, Jesus is not on board with the idea that His message is supposed to be "irresistible" to the world, and that His followers would be known for their "likeability." These specious musings are so opposite from what Jesus actually had to say that, again, the natural impulse is to assume it is all meant as satire, except for the dead-serious nature of its exponents.

So if, in reality, the biblically expected response to gospel presentation is mostly rejection of its message and revilement of its adherents, how then are those adherents to stay faithful? After all, no one in right mind would choose a life of rejection and persecution without some compelling incentive. Without a gripping motivation to remain true, the tendency to defect would be overwhelming. In fact, even during the earthly ministry of Jesus, many of His followers deserted Him as the cost of discipleship began to hit home (cf. **John 6:60, 66**). As Paul writes to the Corinthians, **"If in Christ we have hope in this life only, we are of all people most to be pitied"** (**1 Cor 15:19**).

But it is not in this life that the believer has hope (**2 Cor 4:18**). Rather, faithful followers of Christ are those who have relinquished all earthly attachments, including their own lives, in hope of the eternal blessing to come (**Luke 14:26; John 12:25**). They are those who have denied themselves and daily take up the cross of shame and reproach originally intended for Jesus (**Luke 9:23**). As Paul explains to the Galatians, "**But far be it from me to boast, except in the cross of our Lord Jesus Christ, by which the world has been crucified to me, and I to the world**" (**Gal 6:14**). True followers of Christ are those who have already been crucified with Christ (**Gal 2:20**) and now consider it a small thing to forsake everything for His cause.

Referring back to **Matthew 5:12**, Jesus actually exhorts the maligned believer to "**rejoice and be glad**" for such mistreatment. Why? Jesus goes on to link suffering on account of Him with one's eternal reward. His undeniable implication is that one's experience of persecution is a barometer for how faithfully one is proclaiming the gospel, which in turn brings greater blessing in heaven. In fact, if one is not experiencing any persecution from the world, then one must wonder if he or she is really living a life faithful to the Savior.

Finally, Jesus connects the suffering of His present faithful with the treatment received by His former Old Testament prophets. These "**spirits of just men made perfect**" (**Heb 12:24**) now enjoy the incomparable bliss of holy communion and perfect fellowship with God as they await their promised resurrection (**Isa 26:19-21; Dan 12:2; 1 Thess 4:14-16**). Today's faithful are to look to these heroes of the past, those "**. . . who died in faith, not having received the things promised, but having seen them and greeted them from afar, and having acknowledged that they were strangers and exiles on the earth**" (**Heb 11:13**). These prophets of old—"**of whom the world was not worthy**" (**Heb 11:38**)—desired something beyond this world, "**a better country, that is, a heavenly one**" (**Heb 11:16**), the same heavenly dwelling Christ has prepared for all who repent and believe in Him (**John 14:3**).

So, to review:

(1) Christ's true followers abide in His Word, a considerable challenge given the abundance of anti-biblical notions in today's modern evangelical morass;

(2) Christ's Word promises widespread rejection—not "irresistibility"—of the Christian faith, and widespread persecution—not "likeability"—for Christ's faithful followers;

(3) One's experience of persecution is a barometer for how faithfully one is sharing the gospel message of "**repentance and the forgiveness of sins**" (**Luke 24:47**);

(4) In like manner, one's eternal reward will directly depend upon one's faithfulness in the face of persecution;

(5) Christ's faithful followers are to endure persecution like the prophets of old by anticipating the glorious reward that awaits them in the coming age.

Conclusion
Jesus: The Consummate Polemicist

As we have seen, the Bible is replete with God's warnings to beware attempts of the false to corrupt what is true. Not only that, we have explored Scripture's abundant commands to denounce error as it arises. Paul's instruction to Titus about elder qualifications is one example among many when he writes, "**He** [the elder candidate] **must hold firm to the trustworthy Word as taught, so that he may be able to give instruction in sound doctrine *and also to rebuke those who contradict it*** (**Titus 1:9**; emphasis added). In other words, skill in polemics is a prerequisite for church leadership. Paul then explains why such tactics are necessary: "**For there are many who are insubordinate, empty talkers and deceivers, especially those of the circumcision party**" (**v. 10**). The modern day equivalents of such deceivers are those who would add not just circumcision but *any* work(s) to faith in salvation. And what is the Holy Spirit's injunction against such individuals? **Verse 11a: "They must be silenced...."**

So how is this to be done? Suppose one has been sufficiently apprised of behind-the-scenes scheming of the enemy, of the presence of wolves disguised among the sheep, of demon doctrine in the Sunday sermon, of societal trends opposing the true gospel, of corruptions to God's provision of salvation for the unrighteous, of syncretistic efforts to blend the false with the true, and of erroneous forecasts for the faithful follower of Christ. How do biblically faithful believers apply these warnings to silence today's "**evildoers**," those who are intent on modern-day flesh mutilation with their modifications to the gospel (**Phil 3:2**)?

We need only look to the Archetype of polemics for our answer, the Lord Jesus Christ Himself. On His last day of public ministry prior to His Crucifixion, Jesus gives one concluding sermon to the crowd gathered around Him on the temple grounds, as recorded in **Matthew 23:1-36**. Here is Jesus' final opportunity to instruct the people, a chance to emphasize the most pressing matter for them to remember after His departure. Given the circumstances, it is notable how Jesus does not focus on God's manner of redemption in salvation. He does not review the Beatitudes. He does not speak on the power of God in the life of a believer. He does not discuss His imminent death and resurrection.[25]

No, for His ultimate public address, Jesus chooses the topic which, to His divine mind, is of paramount importance: *false spiritual leaders*. Knowing people must be able to recognize error if they are to pursue the truth which sanctifies (**John 17:17**), Jesus warns them by calling out the false teachers in their midst—the scribes and Pharisees—and enumerating their specific transgressions. What is particularly unnerving about the entire event is Jesus' alarming tone and blunt accusations. In the span of twenty-four verses (**vv. 13-36**), Jesus uncorks no fewer than *seventeen* aspersions against the

---

[25] John MacArthur, from the sermon, "The Condemnation of False Spiritual Leaders, Part 1," Grace Community Church, Sun Valley, CA, March 18, 1984.

religious leaders gathered there, including **"hypocrites"** (7), **"child of hell," "blind guides"** (2), **"blind fools," "blind men," "blind Pharisee," "whitewashed tombs," "sons of those who murdered the prophets," "serpents,"** and **"brood of vipers."** If such scalding vilification from the lips of the Lord seems out of step with the Jesus we commonly hear discussed and preached today, it only reflects how far the discourse about Jesus in modern evangelical Christianity has strayed from what He really said and how He said it.[26] In actuality, Jesus' scathing diatribe models an ideal polemical standard for His followers to implement even today, with four specific principles to emulate:[27]

(1) Reserve polemical broadsides for essential doctrines

The first item to note is the gravity of falsehood at issue. Christ's tirade is instigated by and centers on assaults against a core doctrine—*access to heaven.* In **verse 13**, Jesus says, **"But woe to you, scribes and Pharisees, hypocrites! For you shut the kingdom of heaven in people's faces. For you neither enter yourselves nor allow those who would enter to go in."** Such a serious offense has always aroused holy indignation. Recall in **Malachi 2:7-8**, God declares through His prophet, **"For the lips of a priest should guard knowledge, and the people should seek instruction from his mouth, for he is the messenger of the LORD of hosts. But you have turned aside from the way. You have caused many to stumble by your instruction."** And what

---

[26] John MacArthur, from the sermon, "Kingdom Obstructionists," Grace Community Church, Sun Valley, CA, July 25, 2004.

[27] Adapted from Conrad Mbewe, "Let's Revive the Lost Art of Polemics," http://www.conradmbewe.com/2016/05/lets-revive-lost-art-of-christian.html

is God's judgment against such a despicable practice? **Verse 9: "And so I make you despised and abased before all the people."**

Obscuring God's manner of redemption and thereby impeding access to Him is the most serious doctrinal breach imaginable. By claiming the scribes and Pharisees were shutting the kingdom of heaven in people's faces and hindering entrance, Jesus makes clear the enormity of the error being taught—participation within the kingdom of God is at stake! This is not some esoteric dispute over peripheral matters. This is about the gospel and salvation, about heaven and hell and where people will spend eternity! Jesus knew He came to bring good news about salvation for all the spiritually bereft who would ever repent and believe in His gospel (**Matt 5:3; Luke 4:18; Mark 1:15**). His incarnational purpose was to show this narrow gate to eternal life with God (**Matt 7:13**). Therefore, it is no wonder Jesus concentrates His sternest vitriol against those whose corruption of His message was barring entrance to His kingdom and thus obstructing the very purpose for which He came.

This is the model for the Christ-like polemicist. Not every spiritual difference of opinion calls for conflict, nor is every doctrinal dispute a hill on which to die. God is not pleased with the nit-picking pedant who is always spoiling for a theological brawl. Yes, God instructs His followers to "**test everything**" and only "**hold fast to what is good**" (**1 Thess 5:21**). But this calls for discernment as to the appropriate response when what is tested *isn't* good. Sometimes the better part of spiritual valor is to let an issue lie. When every perceived violation of Scripture prompts a vehement response, one risks being labeled "**quarrelsome**," which Scripture denounces (**1 Tim 3:3; 2 Tim 2:24**). The polemicist who would please God reserves his or her bile for unrenounced errors striking at the core of the gospel and its closely related essential doctrines.

(2) Represent false teaching fairly

Second, it is vital for the polemicist to represent his or her opponent's position fairly. Every criticism Jesus has of the scribes and Pharisees in His extended harangue against them has a factual basis. Aiming for direct quotation is one strategy which can help to avoid misrepresentation; Jesus does just that in this passage, as recorded in **Matt 23:16, 18** and **30**. Direct quotation helps the polemicist stay on topic, knowing that his or her critique is substantiated by distinct spoken or written error.

When direct quotation is not practicable, one must nevertheless strive to represent the other side as faithfully and straightforwardly as possible, according to the Golden Rule (**Matt 7:12; Luke 6:31**). Stick to the facts and avoid assumptions regarding background motivations, then use truths from God's Word to counter the specific error, shunning any *ad hominem* attacks. God is not honored by the twisting of an opponent's perspective, nor is deconstruction of a straw man likely to persuade one's opponent (or anyone else) of his error. Your opponent may descend to such levels, but don't follow him there. More often than not, the polemicist who distorts another's position is relying upon human wisdom and not God's Word to make his argument (contra **1 Cor 2:1-5**), which is a form of sinful pride.

(3) Recognize God's approval of temperament and language apropos to the offense and its setting

The third principle Jesus demonstrates as He curses the scribes and Pharisees before Him is probably the least anticipated: utilize language commensurate with the offense and its scope. This means the intensity of one's reprimand should be directly proportionate to the extent of the error *and* the degree of obstinacy of the one disseminating it. Is the falsehood encountered in an intimate setting? Does one have a personal relationship with the misguided teacher? Has the one dealing falsehood never been appraised of his error? Then go to him privately and correct him gently. This is in keeping with Jesus' admonition in **Matthew 18:15**: **"If your brother sins against you, go and tell him his fault, between you and him alone. If he listens to you, you have gained your brother."**

But what if he does not listen to you? What if the false teacher rejects your correction and continues to propagate his error? The biblical model then calls for increased polemical intensity, as is clear from a survey of Jesus' earthly ministry. Recall early on, Jesus is visited one night by a Pharisee named Nicodemus, as recorded in **John 3**. Although Nicodemus begins the discussion with a benign statement of respect, Jesus immediately pivots to remedial instruction regarding the true path to salvation. The interaction is remarkable for Jesus' audacity in lecturing the supposed finest religious mind in Israel on what God really teaches. Nevertheless, the entire account (**John 3:1-21**) is a model of civility, even as Jesus undoubtedly stuns his visitor with the following:

1. Unless he is **"born again,"** Nicodemus will never see God's kingdom (**v. 3, 5**)

2. Becoming "**born again**" is a process of spiritual rebirth, which happens only by the initiation and activity of the Holy Spirit (**v. 6-7**)

3. The Holy Spirit is unpredictable like the wind as to where He has been (i.e. whom He saved last) and where He is going (i.e. whom He will save next) (**v. 8**)

4. As "**the teacher of Israel**," Nicodemus should be ashamed at not having known all this already (**v. 10**)

5. Jesus claims His testimony is being rejected even though He is divine (**v. 11-13**)

6. Jesus is going to die to save His people (**v. 14**)

7. This will happen because God the Father loved the world so much that He sent His Son Jesus to die in the place of believing sinners, so that they might never die but have eternal life instead (**v. 15-16**)

8. God the Father did not send Jesus into the world to condemn the world because it already lies under the Father's condemnation as a result of sin (**v. 17-18**)

9. Those who do not believe in Jesus remain under that condemnation (**v. 18**; see also **v. 36**)

10. Despite Jesus' arrival and mission, most will ultimately reject His message because they love their evil more than His righteousness (**v. 19-21**)

This is nothing less than a comprehensive and radical rebuke of Pharisaic theology, yet Jesus instructs Nicodemus without any hint of contention or invective. There was no need, for apparently Jesus' words had their intended effect. Scripture does not reveal the specifics of his presumed conversion, but Nicodemus is subsequently seen questioning the tactics of his fellow Pharisees toward Jesus (**John 7:50**), and later even partaking in Jesus' burial (**John 19:39**).

But such was a rarity. Fast-forward three years. Aside from Nicodemus and possibly several others, the majority of the Pharisees and other religious leaders rejected Christ's message and did so with increasing disdain and belligerence. When their verdict reaches its nadir—that Jesus does His miraculous works through the power and under the control of Satan (**Matt 12:24; Luke 11:15**) —Jesus, too, reaches the end of the line with them. He declares their verdict as irrational (i.e. why would Satan be fighting himself by casting out his own demons?) and—*worse*—as blasphemy against the Holy Spirit. Jesus now has a verdict of His own: there is no possibility of salvation for those who blaspheme the Spirit by ascribing His work to demonic effort (**Matt 12:25-32**).

From that point on, we witness a decidedly different tone from Jesus toward the religious elite. At a luncheon at the home of a Pharisee, Jesus pulls no punches in denigrating both the host and his entire religious cohort as "**fools**," declaring them "**full of greed and wickedness**" (**Luke 11:39**). When a lawyer for the religious leaders who is also present objects to Jesus' maledictions, Jesus redirects His ire at him and his group of legalistic scribes. Here again we see the epicenter of Jesus' wrath is false teaching that misdirects the unwary away from God's path to salvation. Note how Jesus concludes His biting remarks in language that foreshadows His later warning in **Matthew 23:13**: "**Woe to you, lawyers! For you have taken away the key of knowledge. You did not enter yourselves, and you hindered those who were entering**" (**Luke 11:52**). Such is the tenor in the interaction between Jesus and the false religious leaders from that point on, culminating in His torrid denunciation of the scribes and Pharisees on the Wednesday of Passion Week.

But—you may be wondering—this is the example of the divine Son of God, who has all knowledge (**Col 2:3**) and to whom all authority has been given (**Matt 28:18**). Do those who are merely His redeemed followers have license to speak against spiritual error with the same authority and conviction? Here it is vital to understand exactly what Christ meant when, in introducing the coming Church Age, He says to Peter, "**I will give you the keys to the kingdom of heaven, and whatever you bind on earth shall be bound in heaven, and whatever you loose on earth shall be loosed in heaven**" (**Matt 16:19**). In this portentous statement, Jesus delegates to Peter—*and to all those who will comprise Christ's body, the Church*—authority based upon the Word of God to speak as God would speak. For instance, in the context of a truthful statement aligned with God's Word, God endows His followers to commend the teaching with confidence as divinely approved. In other words, one can say with assurance that God agrees with what has been said. In the same measure, when falsehood is put forward, the same authority is given to denounce such error; we can say with assurance that God also condemns that falsehood. The question then becomes, is the error a corruption of the gospel and thus an impediment to the door of salvation? And is the error persistent and the false teacher unrepentant, despite discrete and gentle correction? In such a situation, Jesus shows no compunction in excoriating falsehood with invective commensurate with the severity of the error and the obstinacy of its proponents, *and neither should His subjects.*

(4) Redirect your opponent (and all others) to the truth

The final polemical principle we witness from Christ in **Matthew 23** is corresponding presentation of the truth. Throughout His blistering critique of the scribes and Pharisees, Jesus also speaks to the people, contrasting the lies and deceit of false teachers with what is actually true. He tells the people to abide by the Mosaic Law even though their religious instructors do not (**v. 2-3**). He tells them not to be called "**rabbi**" or "**father**" or "**instructor**" because such titles lend toward conceit and do not reflect the intimate, personal oversight and instruction they have from the Father and His Son (**v. 8-10**). He reminds them of the inverse hierarchy within His kingdom, where "**the greatest among you shall be your servant**" (**v. 11**) and "**whoever exalts himself will be humbled, and whoever humbles himself will be exalted**" (**v. 12**). And even as He then turns His wrath upon the false religious leaders, we find Jesus contrasting their mistaken sayings and beliefs with what is actually true.

The ultimate goal of any polemical effort must be presentation of the truth. The Bible says obedience to God's truth is the primary objective for His followers, even preceding love (**1 Pet 1:22; 1 John 5:3**). The Apostle John says he has no greater joy than to know that his brothers and sisters in Christ are walking in the truth (**3 John 4**). No less an authority than Jesus says believers are sanctified—meaning saved and then made progressively holy—through understanding and applying the truth of God's Word (**John 17:17**).

For this reason, tirades against error without contrasting truth are spiritually unhelpful. Notice how Paul follows up his polemical barrage against the false who add works to salvation in **Philippians 3:2** with a corollary description of those who are true in the next verse: "**For we are the circumcision, who worship by the Spirit of God and glory in Christ Jesus and put no confidence in the flesh**" (**Phil 3:3**). Here, Paul arrives at the goal of the searing polemic in verse 2: to establish what it really means to be of the *true* circumcision. Paul's reference to being of "**the circumcision**" is figurative and follows his argument from **Romans 2:28-29**: "**For no one is a Jew who is merely one outwardly, nor is circumcision outward and physical. But a Jew is one inwardly, and circumcision is a matter of the heart, by the Spirit, not by the letter. His praise is not from man but from God.**" In other words, circumcision of the heart refers to the new spiritual nature given by God to all who repent and believe in Christ's substitutionary atonement (**Jer 31:31; Ezek 36:25-27; Gal 3:13; 2 Cor 5:21**).

Stephen addresses this same issue. As he concludes his summary of the story of Israel, Stephen associates the "**stiff necked**" religious elite before him with the wicked leaders of the past, claiming they are "**uncircumcised in heart and ears**" and "**always resisting the Holy Spirit**" (**Acts 7:51**). On the other hand, in **Philippians 3:3**, Paul says the redeemed of God are those who have been circumcised in their heart by the Spirit (**Deut 10:16; Lev 26:41; Jer 4:4; 6:10; 9:26; Ezek 44:7–9**). As a result, they now have discernment to worship God in the truth. Not only that, they now have the ability to glorify Christ in His true form. And finally, they now have insight to renounce any human contribution to the spiritual rebirth they have experienced. Paul's summary in **verse 3** thus becomes one of the Bible's most concise definitions of what it means to be a Christian: (1) to be born again by the Spirit of God, (2) to worship the true Christ, and (3) to reject any form of works righteousness as the basis for salvation.

Commitment to presenting the truth means that polemics in action always has an instructional component, where God's Word is used as the final authority. The Apostle Paul lays this out sequentially in **2 Timothy 3:16**, where he writes, **"All Scripture is God-breathed and is profitable for teaching, for reproof, for correction, for training in righteousness."** Therein lies the role and manner of biblical polemics in a nutshell: God's Word is reliable and authoritative since it comes directly from God, and is therefore useful for teaching truth. The first order of business is its use in a polemical rebuke, or **"reproof,"** of falsehood. Next, falsehood is contrasted with truth for purposes of "**correction**." Finally, having turned from falsehood to embrace truth, one is made for eligible for **"training in righteousness,"** which happens when one obeys what is true. Paul's depiction of God's Word as truth, first for refraining from sin and then for pursuing righteousness, reinforces the words of the Psalmist:

> **Blessed is the man who walks not in the counsel of the wicked, nor stands in the way of sinners, nor sits in the seat of scoffers; but his delight is in the law of the Lord, and on his law he meditates day and night. He is like a tree planted by streams of water that yields its**

fruit in its season, and its leaf does not wither. In all that he does, he prospers (Ps 1:1-3).

Where are Jesus' Polemicists Today?

The words and tone of Jesus stand in stark contrast to the passivity and acquiescence of many pastors and their congregations today in response to rampant falsehood within the Church. Many unsuspecting believers do not even recognize when God's glorious gospel is being besmirched by "respectable" pastors and other Christian leaders. Many are blind to pragmatic efforts to make Christ more appealing and His gospel less objectionable. And when subversion of sound doctrine is finally acknowledged, few are willing to take the next step and rebuke those who persist in disseminating error. As a result, the gospel is under mounting assault, and most harmfully from "friendly fire." As John MacArthur warned years ago, the greatest threat to the Church is not from the outside, but from within.

So to believers on the sidelines of this issue, let me challenge you with the following hypothetical vignette. Imagine a drug dealer sets up shop on the street outside your home. Suppose he is now soliciting the neighborhood children, maybe even your own. How would you respond? It is inconceivable you would stay silent. This activity would represent a real and present threat not only to the well-being of your own family, but also of the entire neighborhood. Failing to do everything possible to eliminate this scourge would be unconscionable.

And yet, as evil as drug abuse is (not to mention its multitude of associated societal ills), the worst it can lead to for an individual is *physical death*. That is the end of the line for the addict. The drug dealer's villainy can only end the physical life of his victim, directly or indirectly. *But Jesus says that is not the worst thing that can happen to an individual.* In **Luke 12:4-5**, He warns, "**I tell you, My friends, do not fear those who kill the body, and after that have nothing more that they can do. But I will warn you whom to fear: fear Him who, after He has killed, has authority to cast into hell. Yes, I tell you, fear Him!**" Jesus knows there is a fate worse than death—spiritual judgment and eternal condemnation. Not only that, He knows a major reason people suffer that fate is from false spiritual teachers in their midst; this is why His harshest words are reserved for such perpetrators.

So now imagine, instead of a drug dealer on your street, there is a false teacher in the neighborhood church. Of course, he doesn't advertise himself as such. He is winsome and cordial, articulate and emotive, funny and popular. He teaches about a Jesus using verses from the Bible. He talks of love and acceptance and getting the most out of life with God. He offers insights into spiritual growth and encourages efforts to serve the marginalized.

But there's a huge missing element—a clear presentation of the gospel, "**the power of God for salvation to everyone who believes**" (**Rom 1:16**). No one ever speaks of God's holy standard of perfection required for communion with Him. No one ever explains how Christ endured the wrath of God upon the cross and why it was necessary to pay the price of sin. No one is ever taught how to be "born again" through repentance and faith in Christ's substitutionary atonement. Nobody carefully and diligently explains **2 Corinthians 5:21**: "**He made Him who knew no sin to be made sin on our behalf, that we might become the righteousness of God in Him.**" And nobody is ever warned what the Bible says happens to those who are not justified in such a manner. One of the great perplexities in modern Christianity is why more people are not frightened at what Jesus says should frighten them, as seen in **Luke 12:4-5**. Were Jesus' followers to have proper regard for the fate of those who die in a condition subject to false spiritual promises and illusions, they would be far more likely to act against counterfeit teachers and the falsehoods they peddle.

The Bible repeatedly warns of false teachers who are obstructing the entrance to God's kingdom, the path to salvation. Jesus demonstrates that when false teachers persist in doing this, they deserve the harshest rebuke. So why isn't more holy rebuke being directed at false teachers within Jesus' church today? There is a strange disconnect when a believer would call the authorities in a heartbeat should a literal drug dealer establish a business on one's street, but the same believer will not even raise an eyebrow when a spiritual drug dealer distributes doctrinal poison in the local church. This disconnect is Satan's greatest success in the modern church. We have seen what Jesus has declared—to poison one's soul is far worse than to poison one's body. Jesus also says it is better to be drowned with a millstone around one's neck than to obstruct those who, in child-like humility, yearn to know God's truth about life, death, eternity and salvation (**Matt 18:6; Mark 9:42; Luke 17:2**). And yet, few hear Christ's warning clearly enough to identify and denounce these malignant obstructionists.

When will today's true believers awaken to the reality of Satan disguised as an angel of light, and his demons as servants of righteousness? When will today's true believers wise up to the ploys of the enemy in altering the gospel just enough to deflect the credulous away from its foundation of **"repentance and the forgiveness of sins"** (**Luke 24:47**)?

When will today's true believers arise to assail the spiritual drug dealers in their community by contrasting their false teaching with God's truth? May God illumine more believers to the clarity and urgency of His Word regarding spiritual falsehood and its perpetrators, and empower them to expose and fight spiritual error in the manner of Christ, until He comes.

Appendix
The Wolf's "Tell"

"Dogs" is not the only derogatory term used in the Bible to describe false teachers. In both the Old and New Testaments, "wolves" is another description used to convey the danger present. In Chapter 2, we reviewed Christ's warning as He concluded His Sermon on the Mount: **"Beware false prophets, who come to you in sheep's clothing but inwardly are ravenous wolves" (Matt 7:15)**. For the climax of His sermon, Jesus underscores the vital need for spiritual discernment, and warns His listeners their main threat would be wolves dressed up as sheep, seeking to devour the flock. His next statement tips his listeners as to reliable wolf identification: **"You will recognize them by their fruits. Are grapes gathered from thorn bushes, or figs from thistles? So every healthy tree bears good fruit, but the diseased tree bears bad fruit . . . Thus you will recognize them by their fruits" (Matt 7:16-17, 19)**.

Successful professional card players strive to hide any indication of the strength or weakness of their hand. At the same time, they seek to discern inadvertent signals from their opponents that might reveal the content of the hands arrayed against them. Such an inadvertent signal is known as a "tell." It is the subtle yet defining tic or characteristic that divulges to the wary and proficient player what cards his or her opponent is holding. The "tell" gives the opponent's hand away. It yields information that tips observant players how to play their hands for optimum success.

As it turns out, Jesus says spiritual wolves have their own "tells," particular features in their teaching and ministries that reveal to the discerning believer danger lurking in the guise of a sheep. According to Jesus, if you become skilled at interpreting the fruits of a wolf, you will become expert at their identification. And the stakes could not be higher: *the risk of spiritual ruin is at stake.* So if it matters to the Good Shepherd to highlight these lupine distinctions at the conclusion of His momentous sermon, it should matter to His followers to remain on the lookout for them (**Acts 20:28-30**).

So, when is a church is being led by a wolf? What are the typical fruits manifesting this deception? Here are some "tells" that may mark a church with lupine leadership:[28]

1. Messages (no longer called sermons) derive more from cultural trends and pop psychology than matters of theological orthodoxy (contra **Jude 3**).

2. Messages are structured more for their entertainment value than for their biblical weight (**2 Tim 4:3**)

---

[28] Some of the following examples are adapted from Kevin DeYoung, "If We All Believe the Same Things, Why Do Our Churches Seem So Different?", The Gospel Coalition, May 15, 2012. (https://www.thegospelcoalition.org/blogs/kevin-deyoung/if-we-believe-all-the-same-things/) and Dan Phillips, "Red Lights," Pyromaniacs, January 27, 2015. (http://teampyro.blogspot.com/2015/01/red-lights.html).

3. Messages feature more quotes from "experts" than Bible verses (**2 Pet 1:3-4; 2 Tim 3:15-17**).

4. Messages focus on human considerations rather than on God's glory (**Rom 11:36; Eph 1:11-12; 2 Tim 4:1-5**).

5. Bible references are from a "favorable" translation (e.g. The Message, NRSV) and are processed through predictable editing so as to remove any potential cultural offense (**Deut 4:2; Rev 22:19**).

6. Believes Jesus instructed His disciples how to be truly good (contra **Mark 10:18; Luke 18:19**).

7. The sufficiency of Scripture is a completely alien concept (**Ps 1:1-2; Jer 23:29; Isa 55:11**).

8. Orients doctrinal stances and official messaging to court the world's approval and avoid its rebuke at all costs (**Luke 9:26; Gal 6:12**).

9. Denies any enduring plan of God for ethnic Israel (**Jer 31:31-37; Rom 11:26**).

10. Committed to theistic evolution, regardless of what Jesus believes (**Mark 10:6**).

11. Committed to earth preservation, regardless of Who cursed it at its beginning and what Peter

writes about its certain end (**Gen 5:29; 2 Pet 3:10**).

12. Is oblivious to spiritual warfare (**Eph 6:12; 2 Cor 10:3-5**).

13. Rejects the concept of penal substitutionary atonement as central to Jesus' mission and to the penitent believer's salvation (**Isa 53:10-11; Gal 3:13; 2 Cor 5:21**).

14. Reveres the writings of ancient and modern mystics and philosophers (contra **Col 2:8**).

15. Believes Christians have much to learn from other religions (contra **Deut 32:17; 1 Cor 10:20**).

16. Misconstrues the "abundant life" Jesus came to bring with ideas of material equality and defense of individual rights (contra **John 10:10; Luke 9:23-25; 12:13-15**).

17. Fails to differentiate between the saved and the lost (**Col 1:13**).

18. Believes what one does for God affects one's standing before Him (contra **Rom 5:1-2**).

19. Believes the prayers and good works of unbelievers are pleasing to God (contra **Isa 64:6; Prov 15:8, 29; 28:9**).

20. Believes one can serve Jesus without "believing the right things" about Him (**John 6:28-29; 7:38-39**).

21. Disregards fundamental biblical concepts such as just condemnation, justification, propitiation, and the need to be "born again" (**John 3:3, 18, 36; Rom 3:24-25; 1 John 2:2**).

22. Considers the distinctives of Reformed faith as antiquated and unhelpful (**Jude 4**).

23. Avoids any public rebuke of sinful trends in culture (**John 7:7; Matt 14:3-5**).

24. Underestimates the holiness of God (**Lev 10:1-2; 2 Sam 6:6-7**).

25. Overestimates the ability of sinners to search for God (**Ps 14:1-3; Rom 3:11**).

26. Papers over doctrinal differences in the search for ecumenical alliance (**2 John 9-11**).

27. Believes the world's response to Jesus impacts His importance and credibility (cf. **John 7:7; 15:18; Phil 2:9-11**).

28. Believes "discoveries" about the world should impact one's understanding of the Bible (i.e. the so-called "God of Two Books" perspective) (**Ps 2:1-4**).

29. When so-called science contradicts a clear biblical statement, inevitably the meaning of the biblical statement is reappraised (**Eph 4:14**).

30. Favors "love" over truth (**1 Pet 1:22**).

31. Sacrifices substance in deference to style (contra **Matt 13:1-9; Mark 4:26-29**).

32. Thinks secular leadership strategies are both helpful and necessary in order to grow the Church (contra **Matt 16:19; 1 Cor 2:1-5**).

33. Insists the message must be contextualized to the audience (contra Peter in **Acts 2:9-40**).

34. Mistakenly believes truth is at the opposite pole from grace (the opposite of grace is *justice*; the opposite of truth is *falsehood*) (**Eph 4:25; Rev 22:15**).

35. Mistakenly (and routinely) substitutes the term "justice" when speaking of mercy (**Isa 30:18**).

36. Believes Revelation is history and Genesis isn't (**Mark 10:6; Luke 24:27; Rev 1:3**).

37. Believes the gospel is not only what Christ did for the sinner upon the cross and through His resurrection, but also what sinners do for Christ (contra **Rom 1:16; 1 Cor 15:3-4; Gal 1:6-8; 5:4**).

38. Derides the idea that one must believe certain doctrinal truths about God to be eligible for heaven (**John 20:31; Rom 10:9-10; 1 John 5:13**).

39. Casts doubt on the existence of crystal-clear fundamental doctrines, or makes much of their putatively subjective, varied nature (**1 Tim 6:3-5**).

40. The gospel is not about personal salvation, and personal salvation is an afterthought (**Acts 4:12; 1 Cor 1:17**).

41. Disdains the idea that saints can know and apply truths confidently from God's Word, especially regarding their own salvation (**1 Cor 15:1; 2 Tim 1:12**).

42. Disdains the idea of "saints" altogether (**Rom 1:7; 1 Cor 1:2; Jude 3**).

43. "What verse are we on?" is totally immaterial (**Isa 8:20**).

44. Gets very excited about radically new ways to reimagine the Christian life, usually apart from any biblical foundation or prescription (**Heb 4:12; Jude 4, 17-19**).

45. Messages show a fondness for creating and then leveling straw men of opposing viewpoints (**Ps 56:5; Micah 3:9**).

46. No one would commend the church for its clear, forceful, passionate, focused declaration of the Word of God (**2 Cor 8:18**).

47. Church discipline is non-existent (**Matt 18:15-20**).

48. People who hate a literal view of the Bible really like this church (**2 Tim 3:16**).

49. People who scorn the wrath of God and the enduring, universal applicability of His commands really like this church (**Rom 1:18**).

50. Unbelievers feel comfortable in this church (**2 Thess 2:10-11**).

51. Teaches that "God is bigger than the Bible" or "Paul isn't Jesus!" which is code for "God sometimes means other than what His Bible writers wrote" (**Deut 4:12; Isa 8:20**).

52. Favors "not rushing in," "taking another look," and "having a conversation" about clear-cut, unmistakable truths of Scripture that violate worldly norms (**Eph 4:14; Col 2:8**).

53. Senior leaders run in a wolf pack (i.e. reference the teaching, endorse the books, and speak at the conferences of known wolves) (**2 Pet 2:1-3**).

Scripture Index

4:7	100	22:11-13	81, 82
5:3	55, 58, 117	23	123
5:5	58	23:2-3	123
5:10-12	111	23:1-36	26, 66, 101, 115
5:12	112	23:8-10	123
5:20	72, 107, 110	23:11	123
5:48	57, 72	23:12	123
7:12	118	23:13	121
7:13	117	23:13-36	15, 115
7:13-14	24, 26, 42	23:16	118
7:15	35, 130	23:18	118
7:16-17	130	23:27	23, 24
7:19	130	23:30	118
8:21-22	27	24:9	109
9:36	55	25:14-30	17
10:22	65, 108	25:34-40	64
10:34	2, 43	25:41	27
11:11	15	25:46	27,43, 83
11:27	43	28:18	122
12:18	50		
12:20	50, 51	**MARK**	
12:24	121	1:15	31, 65, 117
12:25-32	121	1:35	38
12:38	66	4:10-12	43
13:1-9	135	4:26-29	135
14:3-5	134	6:14-29	15
14:23	38	6:34	55
16:1	66	8:11	66
16:19	122, 135	8:36	63
16:26	60	9:42	128
18:6	128	10:6	92, 98, 132, 135
18:15	119	10:7-8	99
18:15-20	137	10:18	132
19:4	92, 98	11:1-11	66
21:1-11	66	11:15-19	66
21:12-13	66	12:1-12	66
21:33-46	66		
22:1-14	79	**LUKE**	
22:9	80	1	93
22:10	80	1:35	43

10:7-13	26	20:28	24
10:10	133	20:28-30	131
11:1-44	66		

ROMANS

11:39	121	1:7	136
12:12-15	66	1:16	14, 31, 38, 44, 127,
12:25	111-112		135
12:48	52	1:18	65, 137
13:14-15	64	2:28-29	124
14:3	113	3:11	134
14:6	46	3:23	73
15:18	64, 109, 134	3:24-25	134
15:18-19	1	5:1-2	63, 74, 133
15:18-25	82-83	5:8	60
15:19	65, 109	5:10	60
15:26	46	5:15-19	92
16:1-4	64, 83	8:1	74
16:7	43	8:5-12	57
16:8	43	8:8	57, 60
16:33	1	8:9	43
17:17	46, 96, 115, 123	8:15-17	62
18:37	46	8:35	3
20:31	136	9:33	83
		10:9-10	136

ACTS

1:15	108	10:17	47
2:9-40	135	11:25	52, 53
2:36-40	15	11:26	132
4:12	136	11:36	132
7:51	124		

1 CORINTHIANS

7:51-60	15	1:2	136
13:48	53	2:1-5	118, 135
14:22	110	2:6-16	18
14:23	38	2:10-13	44
15:1	13	4:7	18
15:5	13	6:3	62
17:25	53	10:20	133
17:26	92	11:1	101
17:28	90	13:1-3	18, 39
18:12-17	68	13:35	64
20:27	36		

About the Author

Colin Eakin is a member of Creekside Bible Church (Cupertino, CA), where he assists with teaching in various capacities. Professionally, he works as a sports medicine orthopaedic surgeon in Palo Alto, CA. He is the author of *God's Glorious Story* and *What the Bible Says About the Future.* Colin and his wife Michelle live in Menlo Park, CA with their children, Hunter and Charlotte.

Made in the USA
Columbia, SC
18 February 2020